LEAN SERVICE

A Practical Guide for SME Owner / Managers

Richard Keegan & Eddie O'Kelly

Published by OAK TREE PRESS
www.oaktreepress.com / www.SuccessStore.com

© 2015 Richard Keegan and Eddie O'Kelly

A catalogue record of this book is available from the
British Library.

ISBN 978-1-78119-177-4 (Paperback)
ISBN 978-1-78119-178-1 (ePub)
ISBN 978-1-78119-179-8 (Kindle)
ISBN 978-1-78119-207-8 (PDF)

Cover image: Felix Pergande / 123rf.com
Cover design: Kieran O'Connor Design

Contents

Figures

Case Studies

Dedications

To Geraldine, Aoife and Maeve, you are my life.
Richard

In grateful appreciation to Jane + 6 for sharpening my understanding of "Best in Class".
EOK

Thanks

With special thanks to all the companies and colleagues who have helped to make this book a reality.

Thanks to Enterprise Ireland for supporting this work.

In a corner of North Wales, in Deeside, Toyota built an engine manufacturing plant in 1991. In this plant, there is a group of enthusiasts, led by Kevin Robinson, deputy managing director, collectively known as the Toyota Lean Management Centre, who have shared their understanding of best practice, how to look at processes and how to build the sustainable capacity of people, processes and business. At this point, Richard has visited the plant 49 times, with over 1,200 Irish managers. The Management Centre's support has been very helpful to Richard personally and to the managers in developing an understanding of what is possible.

Foreword

The global services industry is undergoing dynamic change driven by the development and rapid adoption of new technologies, including cloud computing, mobile communications, data analytics (based on big data) and social technologies.

Irish companies in the internationally traded service sector are participating fully in the opportunities that exist within the global marketplace. Exports by Irish companies assisted by Enterprise Ireland were in excess of €1.7bn in 2014.

The internationally traded services sector is a significant employer in Ireland, accounting for almost 17,000 jobs and so the sector is a key priority for Enterprise Ireland. A significant proportion of these jobs exist outside of Dublin, particularly in the BPO sector where clusters of excellence exist in Waterford, Cork, Limerick and Donegal.

Many Irish service companies have achieved international success with the support of Enterprise Ireland. We have worked with these companies to help them develop capability of their people and processes at home, to approach international markets with confidence. Our teams in international markets have opened doors of opportunities for Irish companies, introducing them to global decision-makers in markets of greatest potential.

Key to success in a global marketplace is the development of Lean principles and practices within processes and service delivery. This book provides material and examples to support the adoption of Lean to develop competitiveness in competing in the global service industry. I hope you find it useful.

Julie Sinnamon
Chief Executive, Enterprise Ireland

1: Introduction

It is clear that service businesses are very important to our modern economies and so it is increasingly important that our service businesses are efficient and effective, too.

Service businesses can be local or global in their nature. A barber's shop or hairdressing salon is obviously a local service, while many software businesses operate at the international, if not global, level. Some 'local' services, such as medicine or dentistry, are now evolving into international service businesses with the advent of cheap air transport and, at the extreme level, the use of long-distance robotic surgery systems, where a patient can be located many thousands miles away from the surgeon. Remote diagnostic services or analysis of scans is now regarded as commonplace in medical circles.

This internationalisation of services can be helpful or challenging to a service business. It can be helpful if you can locate partners overseas where work can be continued 'over your night', allowing your service to be progressed and delivered at maximum speed. It can be challenging if an overseas service provider can access your market, at better rates.

The challenge for service companies is to understand their value proposition, their processes and their customer's needs and wants. As our societies continue to develop and to want / need more services, it is essential that our service companies take on the challenge to develop their effectiveness and efficiency while, at the same time, developing more and better value creation and retention opportunities.

LEAN SERVICE

Lean is about VALUE ... the creation, delivery and retention of value.

The creation of value starts with a resource and ends with what a client or customer perceives as value. In a service business, the primary resource is people. Most services are delivered by people, so a Lean Service business needs to understand its people, how they add value and how this value-adding process can be optimised.

In a service business, the delivery of value is very much customer- or client-dependent. The client defines what they see as 'value', not the business. The most successful service businesses understand this very well and spend much time and effort working to better understand their customers and to meet their spoken needs and often unspoken wants. In a restaurant, not every client wants lots of attention from the staff, not everyone wants the same level of service, and not everyone is pleased by the same things. It is important that a service business understands the core of its delivered value and the spectrum of its clients if it is to deliver its true value.

FIGURE 1.1: MARKET PRICE

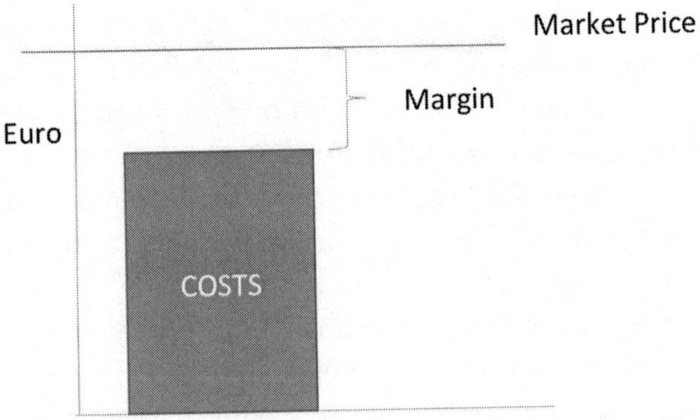

Retaining value is absolutely essential to a service business. It is the retention of value that gives the business the potential to make a profit. The market defines the level that customers are willing to pay for any given service or product. How a business organises its resources of people, systems, processes and premises determines just how much of the value stays with the business.

If you are to identify, develop and retain value, you need to look closely at how your people are trained. How well are your customers' needs and wants understood? How closely are your internal processes aligned to most efficiently meet customers' requirements?

To understand how Lean concepts can be applied to a service business, you need to know a little about Lean Principles, Lean Rules, Lean Questions and Lean Tools. Read on ...

SEEING PROCESSES – LOOK, SEE, UNDERSTAND, THINK, DO

Many managers of service businesses think it is easier to deliver Lean in a manufacturing environment because 'you only have to deal with machines'. This is a commonly-held belief but it is not correct.

Lean implementation in a manufacturing environment is centred on the people and how they interact with the processes and machines. Two different businesses can have exactly the same machines, serve the same business sectors and have completely different business results. The difference is in how the central resource – people – are led, managed, encouraged, directed and supported.

The key difference between a manufacturing and a service business is that it is often easier to 'see' the physical flow of material through a manufacturing process. How can we see the flow through a service business? How can we see where things are getting jammed up, where there is excess capacity for work or where there is overload? Process Mapping and Physical Flow Mapping are the core Lean tools to help us to see the service process. We need to be able to see the process before we can 'understand' it or before we can 'do' something to improve it – but, first, we need to 'look' to start the improvement process.

Service companies typically 'do' something for their clients. Managers in a service environment are increasingly coming to understand that their departments are, in effect, production units. People come in for a service and leave serviced. Data comes in, gets processed and the output leaves the department. This 'doing' is often based on knowledge, administration or an IT approach. The trick for a Lean Service implementation is to find a way to see these processes: to show a physical 'picture' of the processes to let people look for and identify the value-adding, the necessary and the wasteful elements of the work.

LEAN & PEOPLE

Lean is about people, about engaging with people and helping them to release their energy and to realise their potential. Lean Business enables people to deliver real results. The Lean tools and techniques are enablers to help people see processes, identify wastes and remove them. Nobody wants to do a bad job, and nobody wants to waste their time or their effort. Lean in a service environment gives people the opportunity to see their processes.

Because Lean started in a manufacturing environment, it has taken some time for people to see its benefits in a service environment. Many people in the manufacturing world think it must be very difficult to apply Lean in a service or an office environment. But recently, talking to a person who had been implementing Lean in a hospital, she was wondering how Lean would be applied in a manufacturing plant – the wheel has truly turned!

The Lean Service approach is based on two basic, but mutually supportive, elements:

- Lean tools and techniques, and
- The 'Way' – capturing the hearts and minds of the people.

This combination of tools and techniques and engagement of people has been with us for many centuries. The early guild system ensured that members shared and developed the 'secrets' of their trades and equally were committed to caring about what they did and how they did it. The idea of 'caring', where people are committed to 'doing their best' has largely been misplaced in modern business, but it is not lost. The best service businesses are those that care about their customers and their staff, the ones that go that extra mile to ensure their service is well-delivered and well-received.

FIGURE 1.2: HEARTS AND MINDS

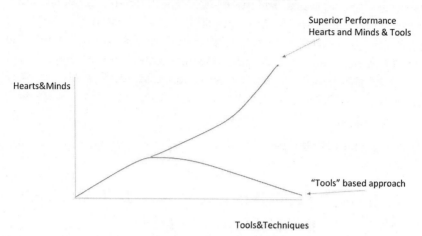

Many companies try to improve their performance by just relying on the tools and techniques. This can be helpful for a time but, if people are not committed to making the business successful, to serving their clients, to caring about what they do and how they do it, then the results eventually will be disappointing. Many such businesses achieve initial improvement from using the tools but this improvement is often lost, as shown in **Figure 1.2** above.

The hearts and minds of our people are very important, especially in a service business. If so much of what our customers see from our service is dependent on our people, then it becomes critically important that our people care about the process, the client and the company. If they are to care, it is important that they are involved in developing the process and service and in enhancing the value delivered and retained. This engagement of the hearts and minds of our people is at the core of Lean Service.

In today's business environment, this combination of tools and techniques and the 'Way' has been rekindled. Toyota Motor Corporation was founded on the core values of its founder, Sochiro Toyoda, who wanted to add value to his society, and decided on the automotive sector as his way to do so. Very many of our global leading brands have similar underlying values, where yes, they are in business to make a profit but they are also committed to add value to their societies, for the greater good. Toyota is well-known for its Toyota Production System (TPS), which created the tools and techniques of Lean, but is less well-known for the 'Toyota Way'. The Toyota Way is about assuring the engagement of the hearts and minds of the people in the organisation and focuses on two key elements:

- Respect
- Constant challenge.

NEED FOR EFFECTIVENESS – WHAT ARE THE RIGHT THINGS TO DO?

Service businesses rely on people to deliver value to their customers. The common characteristic of all service companies is that they 'get things done'. They do something or achieve something for a customer or client.

An accountancy firm uses its expertise and experience for its clients to prepare accounts, manage taxation or provide advice. It might not produce a product but it definitely gets things done for and on behalf of its clients. A software firm bridges the divide between a pure service company and a manufacturing company. Its output helps its clients to do something or to have a specific experience.

In all cases, the effectiveness of our people and our processes decide whether we have a good, profit-making, sustainable business. If our people are not being effective, they will be wasting energy, time and money by not adding as much value as possible to our service to our client.

The first challenge for a service business is to understand what the customer values and then to work to define and develop processes to be able to deliver this value-added service in a highly effective way.

When we have determined just what is valued by the customer, we then can work to develop the most efficient way to deliver that value. We have to understand what the customer wants, needs and values if we are to be effective. We need to know what are the 'right things to do', and then we need to develop an efficient way of delivering that value: 'doing the right things well'.

NEED FOR EFFICIENCY – DRIVING CAPABILITY & CAPACITY

If we have identified the right things to do, we now need to develop the capability and capacity of our people and processes to do them effectively and efficiently. Efficiency of processes depends on both the hard infrastructure such as computer systems, logistics equipment, buildings, and cooking equipment as well as the 'soft' elements such as the level of staff expertise, experience, training and commitment. To develop effective processes, we need to look at and develop both the hard and soft sides of our service offerings.

Developing the capability and capacity of our processes is important, especially with the major developments in technology that we are experiencing today. But equally, if not even more important is the development of the capability and capacity of our staff, and ourselves. Much of a service business' value is created and retained due to the efforts of staff. How can we work together to constantly seek to develop our capabilities and capacity to add value?

The Lean approach focuses not only on the tools of Lean but also and even more importantly on the 'Way' of Lean – the hearts and minds of our people. If we want to be effective and efficient, we need to know what it is that our people need to know if they are to deliver our service consistently and well. We need to know and understand and share what are the things that can go wrong with our service delivery and also know, understand and share 'recovery methods', to quickly, effectively and efficiently fix issues if and when they arise. The very best people in all walks of life constantly challenge themselves to get better, to improve from where they are, to push their capabilities to the highest level they can. We all know examples of top sports men and women who spend countless hours training and developing their base skills. In a practical sense in a service business, we want and need our people to commit to a process of building and developing their capabilities to better deliver true value to our clients and the business.

The Lean Service approach uses a Skills Register (see **Chapter 7**), to support this development approach. The core skills and experience required to do the job is defined and each individual then can map their progress against the Skills Register, identifying what they can do and what they have yet to learn how to do.

2: Applied Benchmarking for Competitiveness

Applied Benchmarking for Competitiveness (ABC) is a simple approach to help service companies to diagnose objectively, efficiently and effectively their current situation and to take steps to improve performance. ABC combines the basics of Benchmarking and Lean Business techniques in a proven, effective form for small and medium-sized companies. Using core Benchmarking and Lean Business techniques, service companies can quickly achieve significant performance improvements.

Using a medical analogy, Benchmarking can be seen as the diagnosis and the Lean Business techniques as the medicine. Benchmarking acts as the diagnosis – an objective look at your business with a view to identifying issues and areas requiring attention and improvement, as well as identifying areas where you may exhibit performance superior to others in your sector.

Taking this medical analogy further, imagine you went to the doctor and were told that, yes, you were unwell, were asked for payment and shown the door. You would have known already that you were unwell before the visit – that's why you went to the doctor in the first place. Now you are still unwell and your wallet is also lighter.

If a company simply benchmarks itself and then takes no action for improvement, it will have made the diagnosis but not taken the medicine. The basic Lean tools and techniques provide the next step:

the medicine – a range of actions that can be taken to help to solve problems in the business and improve its performance.

Developing the medical analogy a stage further again, if your doctor told you that the medicine you needed to take was 1gm of sodium sulphate, 0.02 gm of carbon tetrachloride and 0.001gm of xylene in a calcium base, you would be flummoxed. The same situation exists for a business. It is not enough to know *which* tools should be used; it is often necessary to know *when* given tools are appropriate, and to understand the sequence of their use. Therefore, this book explains:

- Benchmarking;
- The Lean Business tools and techniques;
- How and when these tools and techniques can be used by small and medium-sized service businesses to improve their performance.

By doing this, the book attempts to address some of the key issues facing business today:

- Matching the improvement process to the needs and resources of service SMEs;
- Identifying an effective and efficient transfer mechanism, to help build internal capability in service SMEs;
- Developing an approach to best practice transfer that could form the basis for a semi-standardised approach for service SME development.

The tools and techniques are presented at three levels:

- Basic (**Chapters 5** to **7**);
- Intermediate (**Chapters 8** to **17**);
- Advanced (**Chapters 19** and **20**).

Service companies should master the tools and techniques at Level 1 before moving on to Levels 2 and 3. By learning and using the basic tools of Level 1, a service company will build its staff's capability and prepare itself for the more demanding tools and techniques of Levels 2 and 3.

SERVICE BUSINESSES ARE COMPLEX

A service business is made up of many parts, often dependent on each other. One of the most frequently encountered problems in a service business is that the individual elements or departments are often unaware of how they affect or impact on each other. People don't often get – or take – the opportunity to talk to each other, to discuss the common issues and problems they face. They even less frequently take the time to look and talk about the possibilities they may see or feel that exist to improve the service they provide to each other and or to the end customer.

The truth of the matter is that a successful service business needs awareness and understanding, as well as ability and focused effort, in all areas of the business. One area may be its key strength but, to perform well in highly competitive markets, service businesses need not only key strengths but also need to minimise weaknesses throughout the business.

When looking at a service business, it is important to be aware of this complexity, to understand what is actually happening in it. ABC helps you to do just this, by dealing with the key elements of a successful business:

- Strategy;
- Sales & Marketing;
- Operations;
- Innovation;
- People;
- Finance.

For a service company to be successful, it must understand the interaction of these key elements within its business. If the business has no strategic goal, or has no objective for the future, it can be difficult to motivate people towards success. Unless it can sell its services to markets large enough to sustain the business, then the future will be bleak. Operations need to be able to develop procedures, to build the necessary systems and infrastructure to deliver services on time, at a cost and to a quality standard suited to the marketplace. The design group needs to be able to develop innovative services to meet, and exceed, market desire. The people within a service business *are* the business. Without their skill, effort and flair, the business has no chance of success. And finance, to support the business and to capture a return from the efforts of all, also is essential for success.

A successful service business understands and develops the interactions between these key elements. By doing this, the business and its people will move up the spiral of performance.

BENCHMARKING

Benchmarking is a way of helping organisations to compare themselves against others, in order to learn from others. It provides a proven mechanism to help identify and prioritise areas for improvement within a business in an objective manner, as well as providing a simple way to measure progress over time. Benchmark results recorded today will facilitate measuring what progress has been made in a year's time.

Benchmarking has been with us for many years, in all aspects of our lives. In business, Benchmarking has been widely used in the manufacturing arena, but more recently has been developed to support service businesses, focusing on the key aspects of what makes a good service business. Professor Chris Voss of London Business School has developed Service Benchmarking as a means of objectively identifying both the strengths and weaknesses of service companies as they work to develop their service delivery competency.

In Europe, benchmarking is defined as:

"... a continuous, systematic process for comparing performances of organisations, functions or processes against the 'best in the world', aiming not only to match those performance levels, but to exceed them."
DG Enterprise, European Commission

Benchmarking is used by large and multinational companies to compare themselves against others and to help them in their improvement processes. For small and medium-sized service companies, the issue is not usually about adopting 'best in the world' standards but more often about using current good practice throughout the business.

Benchmarking allows a service business to identify objectively key business processes and the issues within them. It helps to identify and eliminate waste, to find ways, proven by others, to improve performance across the key areas of the business and so to increase profitability and market share. A key strength of the benchmarking approach is that it helps managers to make decisions based on facts, rather than on opinion or intuition. Many management decisions are taken with incomplete data. Using benchmarking, managers can know the performance levels of their peers and competitors and the practices they use to achieve these performance levels.

The benchmarking definition refers to benchmarking as being a continuous, systematic process. Why continuous? What is the point of benchmarking a business or organisation today and never again? Unless a service business continues to monitor progress over time, all it will achieve by benchmarking once is a snapshot of how the business compares with others, at that time. By using benchmarking continuously, it can monitor progress or maybe see none and use this as a stimulus to staff to look for other means of improvement or superior effort.

A small number of key performance indicators (KPIs) can be included in regular management reporting mechanisms to monitor and report progress. Examples of these KPIs could be daily, weekly or monthly sales, monthly profitability, quality complaints, numbers of dropped calls, customer returns or other measures specific to the business. The regular tracking and management of these measures between benchmarking exercises can help to focus people's minds on achieving business and organisational goals.

Why a systematic process? One of the problems with benchmarking is ensuring that like-with-like comparisons are made. Just how can a small consultancy business in the extreme south-west of Ireland compare itself with a digital media agency operating in Berlin? By using a systematic approach, the differences and similarities between business and organisations can be accommodated and normalised. The use of a systematic benchmarking approach ensures comparability between companies, organisations, regions and countries, as well as ensuring repeatability over time. If the same approach is followed, using the same system, thus ensuring the quality and accuracy of data, then it is possible to compare and learn from companies across the world, as shown by the two leading small and medium-sized company benchmarking tools: Microscope and Benchmark Index, both now available for service businesses.

The benchmarking process can help management to identify and prioritise areas requiring change and improvement. In addition, it provides a means of monitoring and measuring progress over time. Modern benchmarking tools have been developed to present results graphically, helping management to visualise relative performance strengths and weaknesses and to prioritise improvement activities.

WHAT GETS MEASURED, IMPROVES

Experience with small and medium-sized businesses shows that they often do not measure performance in many areas. One of the dangers with measurement is ensuring the right things are measured. It is important to know what customers find important and use this as key performance measures within the operation.

The basis of business and competition has changed dramatically over the past 10 to 15 years. The Internet means that wherever you are, provided you have a good data connection, can be the centre of the world. Many services are now provided 'in the cloud', a concept that didn't exist 10 years ago. The worldwide nature of the web means that customers can be served from anywhere in the globe as well as if they were in the same town. This provides both a great opportunity and a great threat. How can you mobilise your capabilities to serve this global market and to defend your business against the threat of mass competitors?

To compete effectively in today's markets, service companies need to be competitive simultaneously on price, delivery, quality, responsiveness, flexibility, and innovation. This is a difficult and complex set of factors and is obviously dependent on a complete business response rather than a single department. Given this shift in the field of competition, European business can no longer rely on simple, traditional performance measures, often used singly.

Seven key characteristics of appropriate measures for this new competitive environment have been identified (Maskell, 1989). Factors should:

- Be directly related to the strategy;
- Include non-financial, as well as financial;
- Vary between locations, dependent on market;
- Change over time;
- Be simple and easy-to-use and understand;
- Provide fast feedback to service providers and managers;
- Teach rather than monitor.

Looking at these characteristics, it is clear that any measures adopted by a small to medium-sized service company need to be chosen carefully. The lack of available time means that, unless both managers and staff can see how the measure is relevant, they are unlikely to use it. This is a centrally important point: unless a measure is used, it is worthless. The information being captured needs to be analysed and used to help improve the process. There is no point in knowing that something is not good within your operation – or even knowing how bad it is – unless you are prepared do something to fix the problem. The Lean techniques outlined in this book can be adapted to improve the services you provide.

WHY USE BENCHMARKING?

Benchmarking is objective. It is often difficult for people to be objective about things they are closely involved with. How can people be expected to be objective about a business where they spend seven to 10 hours every working day? Benchmarking enables people to compare their business to other companies in their sector, of similar size. It allows them to understand what others are doing to achieve their levels of performance and can help them to identify key issues that the company faces if it is to improve performance.

Benchmarking also provides the opportunity to compare a business against international levels of practice and performance. By accessing international benchmarking tools, small and medium-sized service companies can gain valuable insights into how their international competitors work. Given the increasing levels of competition from service companies located overseas, this is very important as it provides a means of identifying real competitiveness levels and also of learning how to achieve them.

Benchmarking also provides a logical way to help service businesses to prioritise their improvement actions. Few, if any, small and medium-sized service companies have spare resources, whether of time or money, to be able to tackle all their issues at one time. Also, many managers are faced with identifying issues in areas of the business they may not be fully comfortable with. Often, managers in small and medium-sized service companies wear more than one 'hat', and can lack the training or experience to identify issues outside their primary area. By using a benchmarking approach that addresses the key areas of a business, they can be helped to identify true issues and to construct actions to address them, in a prioritised way.

A LEARNING OPPORTUNITY

To be a success, it is important to learn with, and from, others. Learning by example, by watching others, is one of the most basic forms of learning. From the days of our early childhood, we learned from watching and listening to others. We learned to walk, to speak and to ride a bicycle from others. This process of learning from others often helped us to achieve difficult and demanding goals.

In the business world, benchmarking provides the opportunity to observe and to learn from others with a view to adapting the learning for our own circumstances. A key point to remember in the business context is that, as children, we often fell down or failed at our early attempts to master a new technique. In business, we may need to use the same perseverance to ensure long-term success.

If a thing is worth doing, it's worth doing badly at first.
Anon.

A clear link has been found between the practices that a business or organisation uses and the level of performance it achieves. The best companies and organisations in the world today – truly Lean organisations – exhibit high levels of both practice use and performance achieved. These same organisations are often front-runners in adopting and developing current best practice. They are, in effect, learning organisations: learning from their own internal experiences, as well as from the shared experience of others.

These leading organisations use benchmarking to check their positions relative to others in their own sector, region, country or on a world-wide basis. Even more importantly, they take every opportunity to learn from, and with, other leading organisations, that themselves are pushing the boundaries of efficiency and effectiveness. A common feature of many of these organisations, both commercial, industrial and public sector, is the belief and realisation that, although they may currently hold leading positions within their sphere of operations, they need to constantly improve their performance across their operations if they are to secure their positions into the future. They recognise the need to improve constantly, to follow the 'Continuous Improvement' or 'Kaizen' route, using the tools of Lean Business to improve their performance, across all elements of their business.

The story is told of Ford Motor Company when it developed a close relationship with Mazda of Japan. Ford had always been proud of its ability in terms of purchasing and materials acquisition and was regarded, by other Western companies, as the leader in these areas. When Ford staff got close to Mazda, they were astounded to see that Mazda used 80% fewer staff per car to acquire parts and components. They were five times more efficient than Ford! Clearly, this revelation led to some serious soul-searching, analysis and improvement within Ford. This practical benchmark exercise led to significant savings for Ford, and a new way of operating.

Change and development, and improving operational performance, are directly linked to learning. You must learn and develop, if you are to improve. You need to learn new things, concepts and techniques, if you are to identify areas for improvement and implement change, or if you are to secure superior performance.

But, change can be difficult. If you are comfortable in your ways of operating, if your company or organisation is meeting its goals, why should you change? You must change, develop and improve, if you are to ensure survival and growth into the future.

When a company or an organisation starts to introduce change, it often runs into resistance. One of the most common types of resistance is the 'not invented here' syndrome. People often can feel that, if an idea or concept did not originate in their organisation, then it is worthless. The counterargument is why must people repeatedly re-invent the wheel? If another organisation has already found a better solution to a problem, why should you refuse to accept it? If you take the opportunity to compare your solution with a better one from another source, you may even be able to improve on that better solution. Benchmarking provides the opportunity and the process to learn with, and from, others.

A key factor in benchmarking is that it provides the opportunity for people at all levels in an organisation to learn and develop. The European workforce is generally well-educated. Remember that the mass production approach developed by Ford and General Motors in the US at the beginning of the last century was designed to manage a workforce that frequently did not speak a common language and was generally poorly educated. Surely the time has come to benefit from the high level of education and intelligence of the workforce?

By adopting current best practice in business, by using benchmarking to learn about these practices and how they can relate to your own operations, by using quality management techniques to implement the changes identified, you can achieve significant improvements in your operational performance. You can measure these improvements with your traditional measurements, such as profit, and manage them with new measures such as lead-time and customer responsiveness.

3: The Diagnosis

Benchmarking is not a new concept. In your daily life, you constantly deal with benchmarks: which is the best football team, which is the fastest car or the one with the best fuel consumption? Your interaction with benchmarking started when you were very young. Were you above or below average height or weight? Were your school results keeping up to standard? Most of these benchmarks were based on numbers, known as quantitative benchmarks.

Ratio benchmarking is based on numbers. However, the numbers alone do not give the full picture and often are not enough to help people to understand what and how they can do to improve their performance. Consider the football example in **Figure 3.1** to see how the numbers do not always tell the full picture – in particular, how to focus improvement efforts.

FIGURE 3.1: DETERMINING THE TRUE SCORE

	Premier Division	P	F	A	Points
1	Manchester United	15	36	12	31
2	Blackburn Rovers	15	27	13	30
3	Arsenal	15	30	17	27
...	...				
19	Barnsley	15	12	40	13
20	Everton	15	16	23	12

Looking at the top teams, you might assume that scoring goals is the key to leading the league table, to being a better team. But then why is Arsenal not ahead of Blackburn? Or you could say that not having goals scored against your team is best, but then why is Everton not ahead of Barnsley? It is clear the numbers alone do not give a full picture of where a club, or for that matter an organisation, should focus to improve.

The numbers can tell only *what* has been achieved, not *how* it was achieved. It is not enough to know that your competitors are more profitable than you are; you also need to know how they manage to achieve this. Qualitative benchmarking, looking at the practices that organisations employ, helps to answer these questions.

Researchers have studied what leading organisations do, how they manage and organise their people, their systems and their assets. One of these studies (Voss *et al.*, 1994) found a positive link between the practices that companies employ and the level of performance they achieve. In simple terms, do the right thing and you will get the benefit!

The combination of qualitative and quantitative benchmarking – looking at the numbers *and* how they are achieved – is an ideal approach to start your improvement activities. Consider a school report in **Figure 3.2**, which shows a combination of numbers / quantitative measures and process insights / qualitative measures.

FIGURE 3.2: IDENTIFYING WHERE IMPROVEMENTS SHOULD BE MADE

School Report	
Maths	75%
English	68%
Irish	80%
Comment: Richard could focus on his English, particularly his grammar.	

The school report provides numbers but also some insights into where improvements can, and should, be made. Understanding how the quantitative and qualitative elements of benchmarking interact is critical to maximising the benefits to be obtained from a benchmarking exercise.

In a business context, you are also familiar with benchmarks: Stock Exchange ratings, financial reports and internal management accounts are well-known and widely-used. The studies performed by Frederick Taylor on the scientific methods of work organisation are early examples of benchmarking being applied in industry. Much of the advances made in mass production were related to this work. Ford, General Motors, Renault and Fiat developed the mass production system based on a simplification of processes, working with Taylor's methods. But, in the early 21st century, we must remember that the mass production system was designed to make *products* effectively and efficiently, with limited variety. The early innovators in mass production were trying to manage a business operating in different competitive circumstances from those of today. Today's managers need to address these changed circumstances, if they are to compete effectively on the world market, especially in service businesses where the demands are different.

Benchmarking is much more than simply copying competitors' best practices. Dr Edward Deming, a leading American statistician who developed many of today's leading quality tools and approaches, wrote:

> To copy is too risky, because you don't understand why you are doing it. To ADAPT, and not adopt, is the way.

The Japanese have used these concepts of early benchmarking to great effect over the past 40 years. In the late 1950s and early 1960s, the Japanese were considered to be the masters of copying. However, they were using benchmarking tools to develop their products and processes more efficiently in terms of time and money than their Western competitors. Operating under a specific set of conditions, they adapted their responses accordingly. For example, they identified logistics as a key problem. So, they identified what was regarded as the most effective logistics operations of their time, adapted the supply methods used by the big American supermarket distribution chains, and developed them to create the 'Just-in-Time' system.

LEVELS OF BENCHMARKING

As one learns about benchmarking and how it can be used to help improve competitiveness in service companies, it is useful to understand how it has evolved over the years.

The evolution of benchmarking can be presented as a series of five steps:

- **Analysis of competing goods (reverse engineering):** During this first phase, benchmarking concentrated on comparison of characteristics, functionalities and performance of competing products. Initially, this was only at a technical level, but was later expanded to include competitive evaluation of products from a market perspective;

- **Competitive benchmarking:** First developed by Rank Xerox when starting to analyse its own manufacturing costs (it found these were as high as its competitors' sale prices!). Now the emphasis is on process efficiency, not just product comparisons;

- **Process benchmarking:** During the 1980s, managers started to realise that they also could learn from organisations in other sectors (benchmarking out of the box). The amount of information and knowledge available amongst non-competing companies was found often to be higher than between competitors;

- **Strategic benchmarking:** A systematic process to evaluate alternative scenarios, to implement strategies and to improve performance through the understanding and adaptation of successful strategies by the partners (competitors or not). It differs from process benchmarking because its scope is larger and deeper;

- **Global benchmarking:** The next generation benchmarking concept, which includes and analyses cultural differences between companies at a worldwide level. It takes into account the conditions (legal, administrative, education, social, environment) that affect the localisation of companies.

Decisive factors for the spread of benchmarking also were the quality award models of the American Malcolm Baldrige National Quality Award (1988) and the European Quality Award (1992). In these quality models, comparisons with competitors and / or best practices are repeatedly requested.

BENCHMARKING AS PART OF THE QUALITY MOVEMENT

Business is under constant pressure to improve, to perform at a higher level. This is as true for service industries as it is for manufacturers or public enterprises. Benchmarking is part of the Quality Management concept and has its roots in industry. Its influence has spread over the past 10 years. Increasingly, organisations like government agencies, hospitals and schools are discovering the benefit of quality management concepts for their areas of operation. Benchmarking, especially, comparing practices from different areas, is helpful and often can lead to considerable improvements.

As for total quality management (TQM), top management support is an essential prerequisite for benchmarking. Without honest and open support of the efforts towards improvement from the top management, no benchmarking project can attain the desired results. In the area of communication, top management can – and must – give the team decisive support. In addition, top management must be prepared to accept less than flattering insights into their own performance capability and to provide the necessary framework conditions for change.

The concept behind quality management tools is about making products or providing services:

"Quicker, Better and Cheaper ... Together".

Each of these words covers a wide range of tools and techniques that can range from the very simple to the very complicated. It is fundamentally important to understand that a company or organisation must come to its own understanding of any proposed concept. It needs to take ownership of the concept and modify and apply those elements that are appropriate for it at the particular time. Companies often start at a low level on specific tools, but become more demanding of them as their abilities to use them improve and their understanding of their power develops. The basic requirement to service customers' needs quicker, better or cheaper is common to all organisations, commercial or state. Benchmarking may have its roots in industry but, today, it is being applied by all types of organisations and businesses to help their improvement processes.

Although most current benchmarking practitioners are companies or organisations employing over 1,000 people, benchmarking can – and should – be applied also to small and medium-sized enterprises. SMEs can use benchmarking because current best practice in benchmarking focuses on processes – when comparing processes, it is of little difference whether an organisation has 10, 100 or 10,000 employees.

TYPES OF BENCHMARKING

There are many different ways to define benchmarking. This chapter already has covered competitive analysis, strategic and sectoral benchmarking. Let's now look at the types of benchmarking a business might get involved with – **Figure 3.3**.

The general types of benchmarking, ranked in terms of ease of use, are:

- Self Assessment
- Facilitated Assessment
- Process.

Each of these tools can be useful and helpful to a business.

Self Assessment is very appropriate for companies at Level 1, when they are starting out on the improvement process.

Facilitated Assessment benchmarking is helpful to businesses at Level 2, when they have some experience in improving their operations. These businesses can – and do – benefit from the input of an objective viewpoint provided by an outside facilitator.

FIGURE 3.3: TYPES OF BENCHMARKING

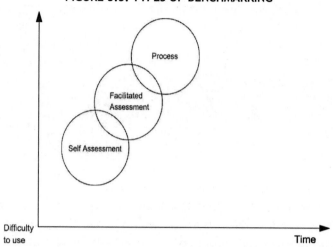

Process benchmarking is often demanding of people, money and commitment and therefore is best suited to businesses operating at Level 3, when they are truly dedicated to improving performance and to competing on the open global market.

Further information on each type of benchmarking is presented in later sections of this book.

4: The Medicine

The 'medicine' is what companies can do to have a positive impact on their performance. When the Lean concept was introduced to Ireland in the mid-1990s, its focus was on manufacturing industry. People thought the ideas and concepts of Lean were suited to – and only suitable for – the shop floor. Since then, it has become clear that Lean techniques are equally applicable in a service organisation, a software business or a manufacturing plant.

Irish companies have used the Lean Business (LB) approach to help them increase sales, reduce purchasing costs, improve terms of supply, simplify and remove costs from administration, improve product development process, reduce capital requirement, manage outsourced suppliers as well as in the more traditional areas of production and supply chain logistics.

Irish companies currently using LB approaches span such sectors as advertising, pottery, engineering, food, electronics, software services, travel agencies, financial consultancy, printing, furniture, joinery, medical devices and pharmaceuticals. They range in size from five people to 200, spread across the country. The usefulness of the Lean Business approach is not limited in itself, only by the vision of those using it.

THE BASICS OF LEAN BUSINESS

LB is a response, based on the need for small and medium-sized companies to perform at the highest level to meet the needs of demanding customers in the face of increasingly aggressive international and domestic competition. The LB approach focuses on providing management and staff of small and medium-sized companies with the tools to help them see and understand their business issues and then to implement responses to address these.

The basic concept can be described as the thrust to make products or provide services: "**Quicker, Better, Cheaper .... Together**". These four words capture the essence of LB.

Why **Quicker**? How many companies have the luxury of providing their service or delivering their product 'whenever they feel like it'? The reality of today's marketplace, with ever shorter lead-times and fierce competition for business, dictates that time is a key factor in a successful business.

Why **Better**? How many customers are prepared to accept quality standards that were acceptable 10 or 20 years ago? No longer is it acceptable to deliver a poor quality service or a bad product. The understanding of quality, as it applies to services and products, is centrally important if operations are to improve.

Why **Cheaper**? Customers and consumers are unlikely to pay more for a product or service than they need to. The pressure of competition has meant that prices for many services and goods have remained at, or around, the same level for many years, when adjusted for inflation, which itself has been historically low. To compete, to stay in business, a focus on costs is needed.

And finally, why **Together?** Experience has shown that groups of people working together can be more effective than a single individual. Most businesses employ more than one person. For the business to be successful, it is obvious that the different skills, abilities and energies of everybody involved in it need to be harnessed in an effective and efficient way. Anything less is wasting a very precious and costly asset.

So these are the basics of Lean Business: **Quicker, Better, Cheaper ... Together**.

But *how* do you do it? The next sections of this chapter will present the tools and techniques that have been developed—and proven – in Irish small and medium-sized companies, to help the owners and staff to use and to implement LB.

THE LEAN HOUSE

The Lean House was developed to illustrate how the elements of LB work together (**Figure 4.1**).

FIGURE 4.1: THE LEAN HOUSE CONCEPT

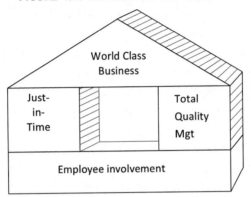

The objective is to build Lean businesses, which can operate successfully on the world stage and which can compete with the best in the business, profitably. The road to being – and remaining – Lean is difficult and demanding. Lean companies will be looking always for their next challenge, the next stretch target for them to achieve.

The foundation for this activity is the people within an organisation or business. Employee involvement presents tools and techniques to help businesses and organisations harness the strengths and abilities of their workforces to achieve a common goal.

To help these businesses reach their targets, Just-in-Time and TQM are used. Just-in-Time tools help businesses to wage a war on waste, across all elements of a business. Although these techniques came from manufacturing, they have been developed and adjusted for the general needs of business. TQM provides simple tools to help identify and monitor performance. These tools work as effectively in a sales, administration or purchasing environment as they do on the shop floor.

The rest of this chapter presents the LB tools and techniques, using case studies based on companies that have used specific tools, in order to describe real life examples of their use. Although each of the companies in the case studies is shown using only one tool, they have used many of the LB techniques presented in this book right across their different functions, choosing tools as appropriate to their needs. The LB toolkit is just that: a toolkit, from which each company or organisation can select the appropriate tools for their needs.

LEAN IS A JOURNEY: LOOK, SEE, UNDERSTAND, THINK, DO – AGAIN AND AGAIN

Innovation in service needs to be seen as a continuous effort. It is not enough to improve things once.

The Lean Journey can be represented as a spiral. The challenge is to move a business operation up the Lean Spiral of Performance (**Figure 4.2**), looking, seeing and understanding processes, thinking about how to improve them before acting to improve them – time after time. As an organisation moves up the spiral, it builds the capability to address ever more important and demanding issues and challenges. It moves to be truly World Class and able to compete on the highest playing fields.

FIGURE 4.2: LEAN SERVICE - THE SPIRAL OF PERFORMANCE

Level 3 Tools & Techniques				
Process Benchmarking	The Five S's	Total Productive Maintenance	Overall Equipment Efficiency	Six Sigma
Business Excellence	Value Analysis & Management	Lean Production	Target Cost Management	

Level 2 Tools & Techniques			
Facilitated Assessment Benchmarking	Physical & Process Flow in the Office	Physical & Process Development	Production Control Systems
Saving Time in the Workplace	Maintenance	Practical Quality Tools	Team Building & Culture
Sales and Growing them	Financial Management	Supply Chain & Logistics	Innovation & Design
Business Strategy	Implementation		

Level 1 Tools & Techniques		
Process Mapping – What are you doing?	Check Sheets – What is going wrong	Teams – People working together to improve
Physical tracking – Where does material or paperwork go	Run Charts – Is it getting better or worse?	

The LB tools and techniques are designed to help a business and its people to: **Look, See, Understand, Think, Do**.

Much of people's time in business is spent handling the 'day job', doing what needs to be done. LB techniques ask the question 'What are we trying to achieve here?' and then they help the questioner to see what is actually being done – the difference between the question and the answer is the gap that needs to be bridged.

LEAN PRINCIPLES, RULES AND QUESTIONS

The Lean Principles, Rules and Questions will help you to understand Lean and to learn how to use it to build your people's capabilities and the competitiveness of your business.

Lean Principles

The three key Lean Principles are:

- Time;
- Money;
- Effort.

Focus on **Time** to see how long work is taking to do, to see how long it is before a customer gets their service after they ask for it. Time is easy to measure and is understood by everyone, so it can play a very useful role as a guiding principle for Lean implementation. How long does it take you to process an order, deal with a claim or provide a required service to your customer?

Money: your business exists to make money, so use money as a key principle to help your people 'see' wastes and to put a value on issues, problems and delays. If you can increase the value-adding ability of your people and your processes, you can rebalance the cost / profit equation.

Effort refers to the amount of work that you have to do to get a job done. Lean focuses on finding ways to reduce the effort required to get work done, to enable you to do more value-added activities, to better serve your customers.

Lean Rules

The Lean Rules provide guidance on dealing with people and processes. Experience has shown Lean Rules to be very helpful in delivering real gains from a Lean implementation effort.

The Lean Rules as they apply to people are:

- **Fairness:** The Lean process needs to be fair, fair to both staff and the business;
- **Firmness:** Once you decide how things should be done, they need to be done that way;
- **Consistency:** Be consistent with how you deal with people, problems and issues.

The Lean Rules for processes are:

- **Look:** Look closely at your processes, go to the place where work is done;
- **See:** See what is actually happening, how things are actually being done to service your customers – the reality will often be quite different to what you think is being done;
- **Understand:** Understand what is being done – what are the underlying principles that affect the outcome?
- **Think:** What can you do to improve things? Can you 'put out the fires' once and for all?
- **Do:** Do something to improve the process. You don't have to make it perfect, just better than it is now.

Lean Questions

Five simple questions will help you to drive competitiveness on your Lean Journey. The first three questions focus on capturing the facts of a situation, while the last two are focused on making things better:

- *What* are you doing?
- *How* are you doing it?
- *Why* are you doing it?
- *Who* is going to improve it?
- *When*?

THE BASIC TOOLBOX

The fundamental Lean tools that are applicable in all businesses, and which should be in every business' toolbox, are:

- Physical Flow;
- Process Flow;
- Check Sheets;
- Run Charts;
- Teams.

Physical Flow

One of the simplest tools to use, the physical flow diagram is very helpful in letting you see the 'wood for the trees', in seeing the reality of an operation or a business function.

The technique maps the movement of work through an operation, whether it is paperwork through the administration area or products through the manufacturing area.

Quite often, processes contain steps that managers are unaware of, steps that have developed over time and which have become part of how staff do things. By mapping the physical movement through the operation, you often can find waste and thereby eliminate it.

Process Flow

Process flow mapping provides a word picture of the processes used. The technique has two basic elements:

- Process mapping of the *theoretical* or 'best' process;
- Process mapping of the *actual* process.

Clearly, the difference between the two is a target for improvement.

Check Sheets

A check sheet is a simple quality tool that lets managers and staff capture real data from operations in an effective and efficient way. The tool is very powerful and easy-to-use.

A list is made of things that happen and, each time one of the items on the list occurs, a tick is placed against that item on the list.

By looking at the number of ticks against each item, it is very easy to determine which items occur most often – and, therefore, which should be given priority in any attempt to effect improvements.

Run Charts

A run chart represents performance over time in a visual manner and provides a very quick and easy way of understanding performance.

The tool can be used as effectively to record sales as production output or quality problems.

Teams

Teams are the foundation of a successful LB initiative. The old saying 'you pay for the hands, but the minds come free' is very true, though the challenge for many businesses is how to harness those minds. Creating and building a team-working environment can be difficult but, when it is achieved, the results can be amazing.

HOW TO USE THIS BOOK

In the rest of this book, these core tools will be described in some detail. They provide a very powerful toolkit to start a LB initiative.

This book is structured to meet the needs of service businesses that want to improve their performance. Tools and techniques that have been proven to work in Irish companies are presented as a series. As you develop your experience, you will advance in the tools you want to use:

- **Level 1:** Basic Lean Service introduces tools proven to be both easy-to-use and effective in operation, which provide a foundation for all businesses, managers and employees, irrespective of sector or size of operation;
- **Level 2:** Intermediate Lean Service introduces tools suited to businesses that are interested in improving their performance, probably those interested in selling overseas, willing to face the challenge of open competition. These tools and techniques will help managers and staff to work together in identifying

areas for improvement. They also will help to focus attention on future possibilities for superior performance;

- **Level 3:** Advanced Lean Service, which has been identified as being suited to the needs of businesses that need to perform at the highest international level, offers a brief introduction to advanced tools and techniques. Although demanding, these advanced tools and techniques are equally rewarding.

As you advance, the appropriate type of benchmarking is presented and explained:

- **Level 1: Basic Self Assessment:** This looks at metrics for performance, based on Island of Ireland statistics, which are available at **www.irishbenchmarkingforum.com**;
- **Level 2: Facilitated Self Assessment:** You use this as your development journey continues;
- **Level 3: Process Benchmarking:** A challenging approach best used where companies are working hard to compete at high levels of performance.

The materials are presented in this structured way to facilitate their use in real business situations.

The basic tools and techniques provide a sound foundation for businesses in general. They must be understood and widely used in a business before moving on to more challenging ones. Similarly, any business trying to adopt / adapt techniques at the highest level would be well advised to be fully conversant with the basic tools and techniques first. Practical experience has shown that, if a business wants to perform at a high level, then the basics of good operational performance need to be secure, throughout all areas of the business, from first customer contact, through design of service, provision of service, administration and finance to after-care service.

The tools and techniques presented in this book have been tried, tested and proven over the past 10 years with a number of Irish-owned and Irish-managed businesses, from many different sectors. This work formed the basis for a thesis, which led to the award of a doctoral degree to Richard Keegan.

Level 1

Basic Lean Service

5: First Steps

When starting out on your Lean journey, it is important to identify a problem or issue for the team that will be both challenging and achievable.

It needs to be challenging enough to allow people to feel that they have contributed to its solution and also needs to be achievable within a reasonable timescale. If the problem or issue is too big or too difficult, then the team may fail, with on-going negative repercussions on future improvement activities.

Silent brainstorming is one approach to finding a suitable problem to be solved, if an immediate candidate does not present itself.

SILENT BRAINSTORMING

Silent brainstorming is an innovation on the traditional brainstorming approach. The process uses Post-It stickers to facilitate the capture of issues facing companies, either at a business level or a departmental / team level.

The process starts with the CEO, MD or senior person outlining the overall objectives of the business and the issues in general that it is facing. Each member of the team is given a pack of Post-Its and a pen. They are given 10 minutes to write down all the issues facing them and the company in delivering on the high level objectives outlined above. Only one issue / item is allowed per Post-It.

Once the time has elapsed (it may be extended, if needed), the team is asked to put their Post-Its on the wall. Their natural tendency is to return to their seats at this point. Instead, they are asked to remain 'at the wall' and to read all the Post-Its.

Once again, their tendency is to sit down when they have read the wall. They are asked to remain standing. They are asked to say whether the Post-Its are an accurate representation of their company. They are then given a further five minutes to add any further issues that may have occurred to them.

The team now is asked to find duplicate Post-Its and to put duplicate ones on top of each other. This usually starts quite slowly. Next, they are asked to group similarly themed Post-Its. The pace of movement increases as the process continues.

The team ends up with grouped Post-Its under specific themes relevant to their company. The analysis of the grouped issues on the wall gives them a basis to develop responses to address the issues and, in effect, becomes the basis for them to prioritise and plan to improve their processes.

The people in the business now know what they want and need to tackle, and now just need the tools to do so.

HOW TO START?

The tools and techniques presented in this section of the book act as a foundation, a base from which to build, based on proven success. The tools are organised to provide a practical, supportive approach to operational improvement.

A business aiming to improve its performance, effectiveness and efficiency should want to progress, but it must master the basic tools and techniques first. Managers and workers will be more able to easily absorb and use advanced tools, if they have mastered the basic tools and techniques.

The tools are presented in an ordered way to help you use them quickly and effectively. By starting with the process flow and physical flow tools, you are focused naturally onto the operations that you know, and are helped to see them in a new light. This new approach to the commonplace usually leads to people achieving early gains and positive results as they improve their own processes and address the 'hurt points' that have been troubling them. This leads to positive reinforcement and a desire to tackle the next challenge.

The basic tools conclude with an insight into one of the key areas of truly Lean operators – people and teams.

6: *War on Waste*

Waste is all around us in business. Not just the normal forms of waste that we are familiar with, such as drafts of documents, incorrectly filled forms, damaged goods or provision of unsatisfactory service but waste in a broader sense as identified by Toyota Corporation and adjusted for the service environment.

When Toyota was faced with the need to improve its operations, it looked at what it was doing and identified seven basic wastes. An eighth waste – the waste of people's energy and capability – was added later (see **Figure 6.1**).

All these wastes add up to non-value added, meaning that effort is put into performing work that is not required by the customer and adds no value.

Not all of these wastes will be found in every service business. For example, over-production is not an issue in a hairdressing salon but could occur in a restaurant, a bakery or a printing service.

In an office, forms of waste include:

- Counting;
- Moving;
- Looking for papers;
- Reworking;
- Filing;
- Sorting;
- Reconciling;
- Checking;
- Duplicating.

FIGURE 6.1: THE SEVEN WASTES + 1

WASTE	EXPLANATION	EXAMPLE
Over-production	Processing too much or too soon compared to what is required.	Producing documents that are not used. Implementing code and features that customer won't actually use.
Waiting	Processes, employees and customers waiting.	Code waiting to be reviewed by one tech lead on a large team, creating backlog and poor quality. Engineers waiting to be asked if they are done and not proactively taking on new work.
Transportation	Movement of items more than required, resulting in wasted efforts and energy and adding to cost.	CCing too many people. Moving cheques in a bank to head office before branches.
Over-processing	Processing more than required where a simpler approach would have done.	Too many project management templates – and all too complex. Slow departmental responses on planning and reports requiring additional chasing emails and follow up meetings to get aligned.
Waste of Inventory	Holding inventory (material and information) more than required.	Boxes of marketing brochures never used and dumped when new features created. Poor management of shared data storage – ordering more space rather than clearing out rubbish.
Waste of Motion	Movement of people that does not add value.	Teams located in different areas, so phones and email used for communication when sitting next to each other would be more efficient. One printer location in company, leading to queues. Travelling to meetings when video conferencing could be used.
Waste of Defects	Errors, mistakes and rework.	Insufficient up front information for a code implementation meaning the engineer makes wrong assumptions.
Waste of Under-utilised People	Employees not leveraged to their own potential.	Engineers bug-fixing other engineers' code. Duplication of work due to poor processes.

Based on definitions in *Driving Competitiveness using Lean*, NSAI SWiFT 11:2013.

In another example, if you analyse the time it takes from the moment when a salesperson takes an order from a customer to the time that the order is delivered to the customer, it may be that the delays in order processing or in generating shipping documents can equal, if not exceed, the processing time or the time it takes to get the goods from the wholesaler.

But what's next? How else can service operations and processes be improved in a practical way?

SELF ASSESSMENT

Self Assessment is the easiest and simplest form of benchmarking. See it as a first step in an objective diagnosis of the performance level of a business in an effort to prioritise improvement activities.

This type of benchmarking is easy to do. All that's needed is your own performance figures and those of your competitors or sectoral averages / norms. For non-quantitative areas, you can answer a set of questions on the practices employed in the business.

However, the difficulty with Self Assessment is the 'self' part. How many people can recognise their own failings? International experience shows that, where companies use Self Assessment, they tend to be overly positive in how they see their own performance.

Nonetheless, given a positive attitude and a will to find ways to improve a business, Self Assessment can be a useful first step on the road to improved performance.

FUNDAMENTAL LEAN TOOLS

The five fundamental tools to help you and your people start your lean service journey to competitiveness are:

- **Process flow mapping:** What are you doing?
- **Physical flow mapping:** Where does information or paperwork go?
- **Check sheets:** What is going wrong?
- **Run charts:** Is it getting better or worse?

- **Teams:** People working together to improve!

These are the basic tools, the first turn of the Spiral of Performance.

FIGURE 6.2: THE SPIRAL OF PERFORMANCE

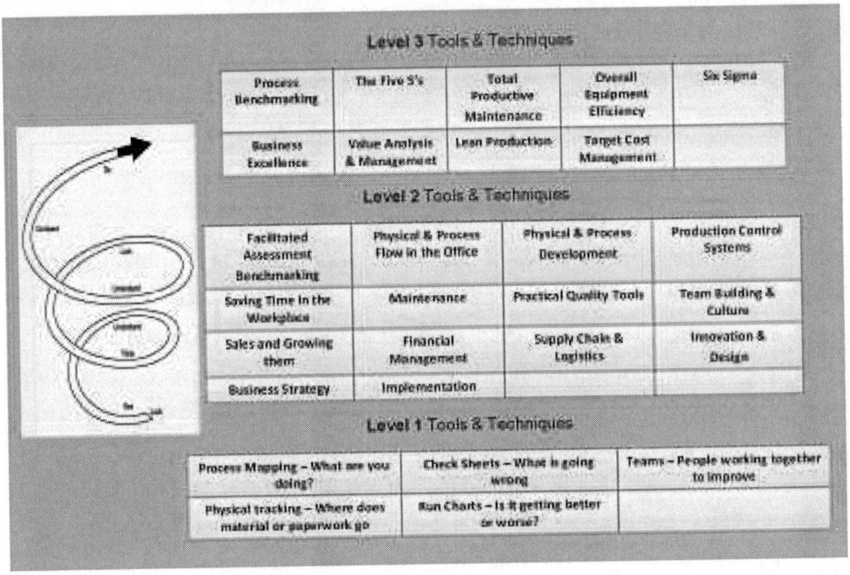

PROCESS MAPPING

"We are a service company, we don't make anything. How can Lean Service work for us? It is too hard to see our processes. It is much easier in a manufacturing company, where you can see the widgets, and how they are made".

How can you use LB tools in offices, when you do not *make* anything there? Although you are not cutting or welding metal, you are processing data, information and paperwork.

The activity in offices can be best described and understood as processes, many of which are common to most businesses, such as:

- Order entry;
- Sales;
- Marketing;

- Accounts receivable;
- Product or service supply;
- Personnel;
- Financial accounting;
- Accounts payable;
- Purchasing.

And then there are other processes that only some companies have:

- R&D;
- Production;
- Environmental monitoring.

Taking the order entry process as an example, let's start to map the process. Remember, you are looking for waste – any action that adds cost but not value. Ask a simple question: Would you personally be prepared to pay your own money for all of the actions that are carried out in the process? Customers only want to pay for the added value, so any added cost effectively reduces your own profits.

Back in the 1950s and 1960s, most managers came from the shop floor, from having 'done the job'. They understood the details of the work their staff were doing because they had done it themselves. Nowadays, however, managers frequently do not have the practical experience held by their staff – we have come to rely more on education rather than experience. In many ways, this has been a positive development, allowing companies to move up the value chain but, in some cases, managers have lost contact with the realities in the operations area. You may think that you know what happens in the office or on the shop floor but, frequently, this knowledge is at best cursory and often wide of the mark.

This knowledge gap is important if you are trying to improve a process. Before you can identify areas for improvement, you need to know **exactly** what is happening. This is an ideal task for a newly-created team, which can map the process in their own areas and, together, build a complete map of the process. At this stage, this exercise should be carried out without judgement as to whether a particular step is adding value. The aim is simply to capture the true facts of what is happening in the operation.

The second part of the exercise is to determine the theoretical optimum process – what *should* be happening. The team can brainstorm this part of the exercise.

The real challenge is to make the actual process used as close as possible to the theoretical optimum. Once the actual steps of the process have been captured and the theoretical optimum has been determined, the team can move towards reducing the wasteful, non-value-added steps. They should focus on identifying the value-adding steps – a suggestion is to use a green highlighter to identify value-adding steps and a red one to highlight non-value-added ones.

Using Process Mapping

Process mapping focuses on two questions:

- What are you doing?
- How are you doing it?

Ask your people to write down what they do to deliver their part of your service, to capture on paper what they must do to provide their service to their customers.

People often ask 'what level of detail should we write down?' or, 'should we use a formal process mapping technique?'. In truth, the level of detail will develop, as people realise themselves that they need more detail to see how they can improve their processes. Obviously, "I answer the phone and do my job" is too low a level of detail to provide any basis for improvement of the process.

Using a roll of wallpaper can be helpful when a group of people is trying to map their shared process. They can write their process steps together, capture samples of paperwork, screen shots and procedures and can effectively create their own process map. The wallpaper can be rolled out until the process is fully mapped. The length of the map often can be quite astonishing and itself can act as a stimulus to action to simplify the process.

As an example, let's look at a fulfilment process – dealing with an order. In an office environment, it's often easier to map the theoretical optimum process before recording the actual system in use. So let's start by mapping a theoretical system for entering an order into the system, as in **Figure 6.3**.

FIGURE 6.3: THE THEORETICAL OPTIMUM ORDER ENTRY PROCESS

Receive order

Enter into sales order record

Check account status

Place order on order picking

Plan into order picking

Pick the order

Deliver to postal / courier service

Invoice

The process looks quite straightforward and logical. Now let's capture the actual process, by getting a team to map and record the steps involved in the process, as in **Figure 6.4**.

FIGURE 6.4: THE ACTUAL ORDER ENTRY PROCESS

Receive order – in Reception

To Sales

Wait

Enter into sales order record

To Finance

Wait

Clear account

To Sales

Wait

To Order Picking / Planning

Wait

To Order Picking

Pick

To Delivery

Documents to Administration

Check paperwork with Sales

Wait

Issue invoice

Wait

Get paid

It is obvious that there are more steps in the actual order entry process than in the theoretical optimum. It is also obvious that many of these additional steps are simply movements and waiting.

PHYSICAL FLOWS

To help understand the implications of these extra steps, use a physical flow diagram. It is an unusual characteristic of applying LB in administration and office or sales environments that it is usually easier to start from the process analysis tool and to progress to the physical flow tools – the reverse of what is done in production environments, where the reality of machines and clearly identifiable process steps make mapping the physical flow the logical first step.

If you now look at the physical layout of the offices related to the order entry process, you begin to see a picture of wasted movement and time, as in **Figure 6.5**.

It is immediately clear that there are very many movements involved in entering even a simple order.

If you now look at the time involved in performing this task of order entry, you could look at time in two different ways:

- **Theoretical:** FIVE minutes actual time to complete the work involved;
- **Actual:** Two to three days' elapsed time for all the steps to be completed.

By putting a time / date stamp on an order, or any other piece of paperwork, it is possible to determine the elapsed time or lead-time. In many businesses, lead-times are often very significantly greater than actual processing time. But what can you do to improve here?

FIGURE 6.5: THE ACTUAL ORDER ENTRY PAPERFLOW

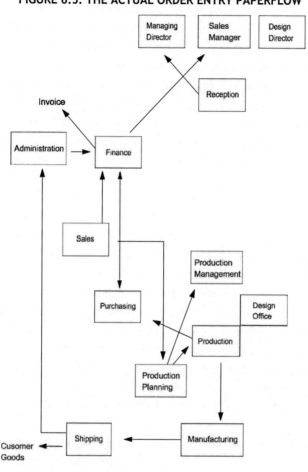

The answer lies in 'What are you trying to do?'. Looking at the differences between the theoretical optimum and the actual order entry process, it is clear that much time is lost and energy used by waiting and movement. Paperwork and information must be moved because the skills and experience required to do the work are located separately from each other. Why not bring task-focussed groups of people together from the different functions? Why not have close links between the different departments – in fact, why have the departments at all? If a work group could be formed around the work itself rather than around department heads, then the job could be performed much more easily. True, the job of the manager might be a little more difficult, having to manage distributed staff, but this challenge has been handled in industry for years.

Sketching out the movements of physical things and information often can lead to questioning why things are done a particular way. A number of years ago when making a presentation to a global pharmaceutical company's Lean team, I was telling a story about a State service provider, where in one of the departments the printer was out of order, requiring staff to go upstairs to use another department's printer ... several times a day. As I was telling the story, I noticed one of the American staff from the company nodding her head. She had the same issue, having to pass through several different departments on a frequent basis just to access a printer. Her boss – who was present – was amazed to hear this and moved to address the issue as a priority.

Physical movement is as important – if not even more important – in a service environment as in a manufacturing one. We just don't tend to see the movements as waste and so we use up our people's ability to provide good quality service to our clients.

The first step in using the physical flow tool involves sketching the general layout of the area under investigation.

The second step involves sketching the physical movements of materials and information through the process. The resulting sketches became known as 'spaghetti diagrams', for obvious reasons. Most processes are laid out in a reasonably efficient way when they are first established. However, over time, and with changes of equipment, addition of new steps in the process or of new people, the physical layout of an office area can move away from the optimum.

A particular feature of the spaghetti diagram is that, at the end of each movement line, there is a build up of work-in-progress (WIP) – a bundle of invoices to be processed, a batch of orders to be entered or a parts list to be 'picked and packed'. In any case, there is a build up, which provides the people working there with a degree of comfort that they have work to do. Managers like to see these piles of WIP too, because they then know that their people have work to do. However, these piles of WIP are costly, in terms of time to process jobs as well as in terms of cash. To show this, at each location on the sketch, simply note the value, in Euro, of the paperwork (invoices, orders, bills) or materials in the packaging area.

The key objective of the physical process flow exercise is to find ways to remove, or at least reduce, movements from the process. A useful measure in an office environment can be how many pages of paper are moved how many kilometres around the office each year? The answer in most offices is in the order of millions – sometimes, billions – of page-kilometres per year. Obviously, no customer willingly pays for this movement of paper, so who is paying for it? The business is – it pays for these wastes of movement through a reduced profit margin. Lost profit is what pays for these wasteful page-kilometres.

FIGURE 6.6: ADMINISTRATION - TRADITIONAL

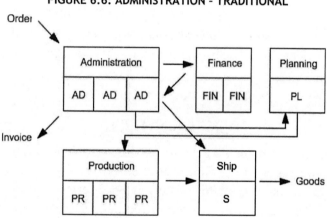

The diagrams above and below (**Figures 6.6** and **6.7**) show the difference between the traditional and LB arrangements in an administration setting. The simple fact of grouping people together, around the task at hand (the process), leads to the opportunity for increased effectiveness and efficiency. People begin to see how they relate to each other; physical movement is reduced significantly; and waiting time practically disappears. Because all the team members are aware of what is happening in the operation, they are able to support each other and have a peripheral awareness of what jobs are coming at them next. This awareness leads to preparedness and increased operational performance.

FIGURE 6.7: ADMINISTRATION - LEAN BUSINESS

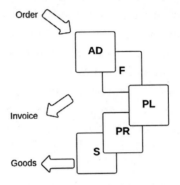

The close links between the physical flow and process flow tools should be clear now. Together, they can help highlight improvement opportunities.

CHECK SHEETS

You need to improve. You want to improve. What is holding you back? If you ask staff for the cause of delays in providing service to customers, or the reasons for defects or poor service, quite often the reason given is not the real reason for poor performance. It is an 'opinion', not a 'fact'. But it is often difficult to remember why a report or a transaction was delayed. It is very difficult to try to improve processes without having the facts of what the 'hurt points' actually are, those things that make it difficult for us to do our jobs right, first time.

The check sheet is one of the simplest quality tools – and one of the most powerful. When faced with the task of improving a process, the challenge is often in knowing what is actually happening as the process runs – what are the facts of the situation rather than people's opinions, since opinions and instinct can be wrong. The check sheet provides a simple way to record the facts of the situation.

If you are looking to improve a sales operation, some basic facts are needed:

- Who is buying what?
- When?
- In what quantities?
- From which sales people?

If your focus is on improving an administration group's effectiveness and efficiency, it is probably important to know:

- Who is accurate in their work and who is not?
- What types of interruptions occur?
- At what frequency?
- How long do these interruptions typically last?

The answers to these and many other questions are easily captured using check sheets. A check sheet captures facts without imposing a significant workload, by recording, using a simple mark on the sheet, the number and types of errors in a process or in a service.

When developing a check sheet, consider:

- What is to be recorded?
- Over what time period?
- Who will record the data?
- Who will act on the data to improve the process?

The fourth question above is arguably the most important. If time and energy are spent in capturing and recording data, then action to improve the process afterwards is necessary. Otherwise, the exercise is simply an additional waste. As an example, let's look at an administration case in **Figure 6.8,** where a check sheet captures data on the process.

By looking at the check sheets for all staff in the group, you can determine whether there are problems with telephone-answering or the handling of visitors. Any improvements then can be based on facts.

FIGURE 6.8: ADMINISTRATION CHECK SHEET

Telephone	||||| ||||| ||||| ||
Visitor	|||||	
E-Mail	||||| ||||| |||
New Query	||
Rework	||||
Other	|||
Person	J Murphy
Date	4/04/2012

Experience has shown that six to seven items per check sheet – one of which should be 'Other' – is an optimum. Obviously, if 'Other' has lots of marks recorded against it, the list needs to be developed further to capture more useful information.

In analysing the data from a check sheet, do not assume that, because something happens most frequently, it is the most important problem – it is merely the most frequent and certainly, because of that, deserving of attention. But one must gauge the impact of each fault to determine what, in fact, are the key issues identified by the check sheet.

Using a Check Sheet to Capture Hurt Points

Many people are frustrated in their work. They don't have all the information they need to complete a task or they don't have all the right information.

Very often, the people who provide the information are not aware of the 'hurt' they are causing their colleagues. Using a check sheet to dispassionately record when something is not right gives people working in the process a clear voice, to help themselves to be heard. Very few people set out to do a bad job or to make life difficult for their colleagues. Because the check sheet gives the basic facts of what is happening in a process, it provides a way to help share with each other where the hurt points are so that they can be addressed and removed, together.

RUN CHARTS

A run chart presents trends over time. If an improvement process is underway, you hope to see improvement over time, either in increased productivity or sales or in reduced complaints or whatever measurement is appropriate. Many companies do not record their performance over time – in effect, every day is 'another day in the mines' for their staff. There is no means of knowing whether their performance is getting better, staying the same, or even deteriorating. Run charts can be used to monitor performance in areas that are important to the business.

If customers value response time, or accuracy in paperwork, performance in these areas should be measured over time. These measures then should be made available to the people who can affect change.

> There is no harm in letting people see what they have done –
> and what they have to do.
> **Denis Keegan**

On a more positive note, if people have been working to improve a process, they will be able to see an improvement in performance on the run chart. This can act as a very positive reinforcement for the team.

As an exercise, see whether you can visualise what the numbers in **Figure 6.9** show.

Then look at the same data presented in a run chart, in **Figure 6.10**, where changes in performance can be seen clearly. If performance deteriorates, then questions can be asked to find out why.

The run chart can be further developed as a challenge to the team. The addition of a target line will give the team an objective, and also the means to measure progress towards this objective, as in **Figure 6.11**.

FIGURE 6.9: NUMERIC DATA CAPTURE

Fill No	Date	Km	Sum Km	Litres	Station	€	
1	30-Oct			21.7	ST	11.98	
2	02-Nov	277	277	20.8	E	11.42	37.1
3	05-Nov	285	562	21	T	12.53	37.8
4	09-Nov	250	812	20.2	ST	11.17	34.5
5	11-Nov	267	1079	19.2	E	11.36	38.7
6	14-Nov	312	1391	20.8	ST	12.67	41.8
7	24-Nov	218	1609	21	E	11.57	28.9
8	25-Nov	304	1913	20	T	11.99	42.3
9	03-Dec	244	2157	19.5	SH	11.51	34.8
10	04-Dec	253	2410	16.4	E	10.14	42.9
11	04-Dec	340	2750	21.8	E	12.08	43.4
12	09-Dec	272	3022	20.7	ST	12.05	36.6
13	17-Dec	268	3290	21.6	E	11.72	34.5
14	22-Dec	198	3488	19.4	ST	10.46	28.4
15	02-Feb	221	3709	20.9	E	11.26	29.4
16	03-Feb	291	4000	20.3	E	10.77	39.9
17	03-Mar	208	4208	20	E	10.55	29.0
18	16-Mar	217	4425	20.2	ST	10.38	29.9
19	23-Mar	255	4680	19.3	T	10.98	36.8
20	25-Mar	269	4949	19.7	SH	10.78	38.0
21	13-Apr	242	5191	21	E	12.4	32.1
22	15-Apr	259	5450	20	T	12.07	36.0
23	15-Apr	270	5720	19.4	T	11.07	38.7
24	16-Apr	251	5971	19.8	M	10.9	35.3

FIGURE 6.10: MILES PER GALLON - RUN CHART

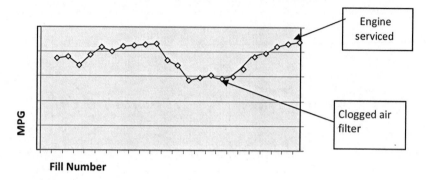

FIGURE 6.11: MILES PER GALLON - RUN CHART WITH TARGET LINE

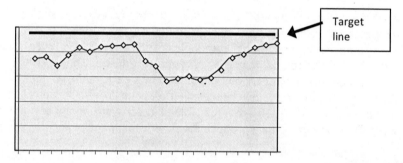

Using run charts with target lines, and highlighting key actions taken to secure improvement, also may help to develop an innovation culture in the business. The ever-present challenge is to ask what can be done next to bridge the gap between present and potential performance.

Case Study 1: Applying Lean Principles in Openet

Openet is a privately-owned Irish software company, employing over 900 people globally. We specialise in providing business support systems to telecom and communications companies and among our clients we number five of the top 10 telcos by revenue worldwide. The software we produce processes tens of billions of transactions each day and does so in real-time with extremely low latencies, measured in milliseconds. Over 700 of the Openet staff are actively involved in software engineering, with around 300 working on core product development alone.

Why Lean?

We have always been focused on best practices and methodologies in pursuit of the highest quality software and, as part of our on-going evolution and as part of our scaling programme, we launched in 2010 a programme to implement Lean processes in software engineering. As with many software houses, the journey to Lean has passed through distinct phases denoted by specific popular software methodologies. Our route went from the prevailing Waterfall methodology through Scrum (or, in our case, what we affectionately called 'Watergile'), to Agile and Scrumban and we march onwards to our goal of a fully Kanban-based 'pull' system.

Retrospectively, and indeed on an on-going basis, our experience broadly can be broken down into two separate parts:

- The social change management encompassing the challenge of changing the mindset of hundreds of engineers who have spent a lifetime working in a very different way;

- The process and discipline changes encompassing the application of the Lean principles: eliminate waste; amplify learning; decide as late as possible; deliver as fast as possible; empower the team; and build integrity in.

Though the process part proved much the simpler of the two, both in terms of ease of measurement and of implementation, the first proved to be the more challenging but probably most rewarding as observing the conversion of a sceptic to an evangelist is an amazing thing and the power for that evangelist to effect change is remarkable.

If You Can't Measure, You Can't Improve
The single biggest challenge we faced was that there was a lack of valid metrics being gathered consistently in the organisation, both inside of development teams and across the engineering group. Our discipline in terms of gathering measurements and tracking them was not what it needed to be. Indeed, were the whole of the Lean program to stall save for the instilling of a measurement culture, I would argue that it was a success.

As we began to measure, we began to learn. When people began to see the measurements they were taking begin to yield tangible learnings, it fuelled a virtuous cycle wherein the more care and attention was taken with the measurements the higher the yield in learning and more improvement. While we still struggle with defining a 'standard unit of work' across the whole organization, we do see on a team-by-team basis better and better accuracy in estimation and completion.

Initially, we focused in the programme on two key metrics:

- 'Commit Diligence' or how close you were to the estimate you provided;

- 'Velocity' or the volume of work delivered in the time measured.

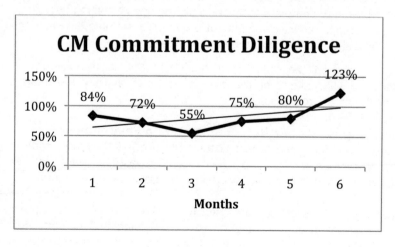

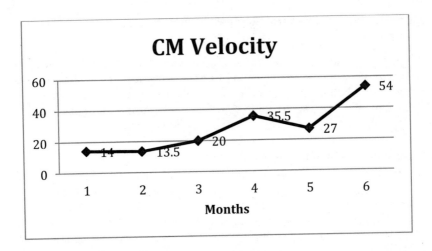

Both of these measures contribute in a major way to providing 'flow' or smooth passage through the process. As we properly estimate the size and prioritise the work, we remove much of the waste inherent in much software development cycles.

Moving beyond this, we have identified further measures that bring even more clarity to the value of the work we do:

- **'Found Work'** is the work discovered as we progress through a cycle that adds time but delivers real benefit greater than if it were ignored or moved to a later point in our development. It may delay the deliverable in the short-term or cause another item to be de-scoped but its value to the customer and the project is greater;

- **'Focus Factor'** is a measure of the interruptions to the team while attempting to complete the work. This may be correcting bugs discovered in earlier shipments or provision of training time as a result of deficiencies in our documentation or usability.

These metrics will be continuously added to and as they become fully understood will cease to be the focus of attention as they are automated and built into the processes.

Identifying Waste in a Non-manufacturing Environment

If I were to choose one aspect of the Lean process that most confounds software engineers, it would be the concept of waste as described in Lean as there is effectively no inventory, no transportation, no motion (save perhaps RSI and eye-strain!) and no cost to overproduction. So we software engineers often fail to see the waste inherent in the process. While 'waiting' is obvious enough, overprocessing and defects are the bane of the software industry and it is here we can generate the most savings or inject the most value. Automation of testing and continuous integration being built into the process are vital steps to realising the goals of not sending defective products to the subsequent process or the customer.

Key to our focus on waste has been a change to how we describe the work that we are to do, moving it from the 'how' and the 'what' (technical) to the 'why' (what benefit accrues to the customer). We continue to evolve this work and, with each iteration, we get closer to defining everything from a customer value perspective, eliminating work that does not benefit the customer. With respect to process change, we focus on what steps in the chain are providing the most / least value and look to tweak these, continuously improving as we move along.

What we have learned over the last two years is that, while we have been very successful as a company and as a team of engineers, we know now – and can show – that we are not nearly as efficient as we could be and that we can achieve huge improvements entirely by modifying things within our own control. These changes are being made without diverting resources from our day-to-day work and are actively contributing to both the control of bottom-line growth and increase of top-line revenue in terms of the company's success.

The most remarkable thing about software development globally with respect to Lean practices is that it has taken so long for it to catch on at all. As with many sectors that are not manufacturing physical goods, the software industry eschewed Lean as a 'factory line' process not applicable to a 'knowledge-based' business. Having spent the last three years working the Lean principles into our methodology, we can attest to how wrong we are as a sector to ignore it and how tangible and valuable the learning has been. While we are a long way from the end, each step on the way is further enhancing our business and delivering on our dual goals of delighting our customer and having happier staff.

7: Teams & People

The Lean approach places an emphasis on teams and team-working, which is essential in today's highly competitive environment, where the power of a well-functioning team can be the difference between success and failure. Most companies can afford to buy or lease good equipment. The difference between successful and unsuccessful companies often lies in how well they use these assets. The people working in a business or organisation add the value to its services. In the developing knowledge-based economic environment, businesses that harness the potential of their people will thrive, while those that do not will find it difficult to survive. We know this harnessing of individuals as building teams.

There are clear and effective ways of bringing people together, to work together, for a common objective. This is the central point in relation to team-building – people need to have a common objective, a reason to work as a team, a goal. One can often see volunteers doing work, for free, that they would never do if they were being paid, because they are working to achieve an objective, a shared goal.

In the Lean Service environment, three words explain the engagement of staff, working together:

- Respect;
- Accept;
- Expect.

Lean is fundamentally based on respect for people. This respect works in many directions, at the same time. Managers need to respect their staff. Staff need to respect their managers. Staff and managers both need to respect the business and, at the heart of all service businesses, the customer needs to be respected and serviced effectively and well and at an acceptable level of quality.

It is also important to set out clearly what is acceptable, what the business accepts as an appropriate level of service or conduct or manners. People need to know what they can and cannot do. They need to know what is regarded as acceptable for interactions between the company, colleagues and customers.

And finally, people need to know what is expected of them. In the Lean Service environment, this usually means that they are expected to do a good job as well as helping to make the 'job' better, all the time. This is quite a challenge and can be very powerful when a group of people decides to become a team. In short, people need to decide to engage and to be motivated in their work.

Tools and techniques are important but, if they are to benefit a business, they need to be used and implemented by people. Business depends on people. People work the systems and processes and computers that deliver customer needs. People need to be managed and to be involved in the improvement process, in order to maximise their contribution to the business. People need to be respected and appreciated by their businesses and their management. People need to be led and to participate in a process.

This chapter looks at some basic techniques to start this process of building people-power and capability, based always on mutual respect, trust and effort.

THE SKILLS REGISTER – WHO HAVE YOU GOT AND WHAT CAN THEY DO?

The Lean approach places an emphasis on teams and team-working. All teams are made up of individuals, with different abilities, personalities and experience levels. To develop a fully-capable team means identifying:

- What skills and experience are required by the business?
- Who has it available on staff?

- What is their level of capability in relation to the required skills set?

The skills, experiences and expertise of the people in a business will define the quality of the service offering. But how can a business develop its people to allow it to operate at the highest levels of performance? It can be very difficult to identify individuals' abilities objectively. The Lean approach provides a tool known as the skills register to help with this process. An example of a skills register for administration and customer support is presented in **Figure 7.1**.

FIGURE 7.1: SKILLS REGISTER

Job Details	Telephone		Computer Skills			Administration		Other Skills
	Answer	Transfer	Word	Excel	System	Order Entry	Customer Complaints	
Richard								
Paddy								
Mary								
Joan								

Job Area: Administration and Customer Support

Each staff member has a four-box square under each of the key job skill areas. The skill level of each staff member is represented by the number of filled boxes. The standard interpretation of the skills register is usually as follows:

- **No boxes:** Staff member is untrained or unskilled in this area;
- **One box:** A basic introduction to the topic has been given;
- **Two boxes:** Staff member is able to perform the task, under supervision and with support;

- **Three boxes:** Staff member is largely capable of performing the task, although they may require some support and light supervision;
- **Four boxes:** Staff member is fully capable.

The system is very simple: gaps in skills are easily seen and recognised and then can be addressed.

Extend the skills register by capturing in the 'Other Skills' column any skills that staff have that are not directly related to their current job. You may have staff with significant skills and experience that you are not currently availing of.

The skills register is often used on an individual basis as part of a personal development plan and also can be used in a more general way where the register is displayed in team meeting areas. This approach can be helpful where team members realise they have gaps in their skills that they can take training for.

WHY PEOPLE WORK TOGETHER

For people to work together as a team, there needs to be a reason to do so. Just bringing people together and calling them a team will not deliver teamwork. It is essential that a real reason exists, or is created, for them to work together. Without this reason, they will continue to work as they had before – as individuals. The introduction of a shared objective, one that cannot be achieved by individual action, is useful to get the attention of all concerned.

A key factor for success, when trying to form a team in a business environment, is that management shows an on-going interest in the activities, progress and results of the team. Unless people see that their efforts are both significant and important, they are unlikely to put much effort into developing this alien form of working. On the other hand, if management shows an interest in the effort, monitors progress and introduces measures to ensure team-working is happening, people will respond and deliver.

TEAM-BUILDING

There is a lot known about the detail of team-building. Many larger organisations and businesses employ such techniques as psychometric profiling, personality profiling and other psychological tools and techniques to ensure they have a good mix of characteristics in a team. Most small and medium-sized companies do not have this luxury, and have a restricted pool of people to choose from.

So, is it possible to form effective teams without using the specialist tools and techniques? The answer is Yes! Once the reason for the team to exist has been identified, and the objective that needs to be reached has been set, the process of team-building can begin. However, on a practical note, it is important to recognise that not everybody is able or suited to working in a team environment. Some people find it very difficult to interact with others. A decision must be made as to whether such individuals have a positive role to play within the organisation, working on their individual tasks, or whether their best opportunities lie outside the organisation. These can be difficult decisions for all concerned.

DIFFERENT TYPES OF PEOPLE

People in general fall into a number of categories:

- **Type A:** Those who are inherently positive, who will try to deliver, who will take on new challenges and new ideas. These account for about 10% of a workforce;

- **Type B:** The main body of people in a workforce, at both management and operational levels, accounting for about 85% of the workforce. These people want to see how things will work out before they commit to a new way of working. When, and if, they see the new way working, they are usually happy to join in;

- **Type C:** The negative group, those who always seem to say, "That won't work!". Quite often, these are experienced people, with lots of skill and ability. Maybe they are right, maybe the new way won't work, because they have seen a serious flaw. Maybe they also see a solution to the flaw! This can be a hard group to win over but also a very rewarding one. Unfortunately, experience has shown that while many within this group can – and do – change to become positive contributors, some of these people find it impossible to embrace change and generally tend to pursue alternative careers.

Most people are self-motivated. They drive themselves to perform at a level that they want to perform at. Rich Teerlink was managing director of Harley-Davidson (H-D) at a very interesting time in its history. H-D makes motorcycles, and had just come out of administrative protection when Teerlink took over. In his book, *More than a Motorcycle,* he describes his journey. He wondered how he could motivate thousands of disparate H-D staff, from directors to floor-sweepers. He asked himself what he wanted from his job – and answered:

- To do a good job;
- To get reasonably well paid for doing it;
- To be happy that the job would continue into the future.

When he asked his fellow senior managers why they worked, they all came up with more or less the same three points. He continued to ask staff throughout the organisation and, while they often used different words, they all expressed the three same points. Ask yourself the question? Do you give the same three answers?

People want to do a good job, and be recognised for it. They want to get paid reasonably well for doing so, and they want to have the security of believing that the job will continue. If this is a common thread, then there is indeed a common link between all the people working in a business. This is, in fact, our motivation.

This approach helps us understand the interfaces between extrinsic rewards, such as wages, bonuses and awards, and intrinsic rewards, such as self-respect from doing a good job and being part of something bigger than just yourself.

SO, WHERE TO START?

As noted earlier, it is important to identify a problem or issue for the team that will be both challenging and achievable. It needs to be challenging enough to allow people to feel that they have contributed to its solution and also needs to be achievable within a reasonable timescale. If the problem or issue is too big or too difficult, then the team may fail, with on-going negative repercussions on future improvement activities.

Once the issue or problem has been identified, the next task is to identify who should be on the team. We will deal later with the selection of team members, at this point we are dealing only with the types of people to be on the team: A, B or C.

Practical experience has shown that the first efforts at team-building are the most important. If you are introducing team-working to help an improvement initiative, it is probably best to pick positive, Type A people, with some Type B 'wait and see' people, in the early teams.

Some experts suggest including Type C people, the 'nay-sayers', in early teams, on the basis that if they can be won over through the success of the team a major obstacle will have been removed. However, often this is not the most effective approach. It is usually better to achieve success with a positive or neutral group of people rather than trying to convince the 'nay-sayers' to change their attitude.

THE FACILITATOR

Team-working can be a new way of working for many people. How do they do it? How is it different from what went before? These and many more questions can – and do – arise.

A facilitator can be very helpful when introducing team-working, providing answers to many questions and helping people to come to terms with the new approach. The facilitator can be a member of staff or an outsider. Either approach can be successful.

Many companies and organisations choose to use an external facilitator in the early stages, taking the opportunity to learn from experienced people and also maybe to benefit from somebody outside the organisation 'breaking the ice'. The outsider often can raise issues and questions that would be difficult for someone within the operation to do. This can be particularly useful where deep-seated issues exist.

The role of the facilitator can be difficult and is frequently taxing, as they have to retain a degree of separation from the company and the issues, while concentrating very closely on them and the team process to help ensure a positive outcome. The facilitator has been likened to a catalyst in a chemical reaction, not strictly necessary for the reaction to take place but helpful in ensuring the result and speeding the process (in chemistry, a catalyst helps bring about change without being changed itself).

Once the general objective and goals of the team have been identified and the team members selected, typically the facilitator's role involves:

- Leading the first team meeting;
- Helping the team to select detailed projects to deliver on the objectives;
- Starting the process of open discussion;
- Ensuring that all team members get the opportunity to contribute;
- Letting the team set its own priorities;
- Moving away by devolving power and authority to the team;
- Monitoring the progress of the team towards its objectives;
- Praising and reinforcing achievements;
- Identifying areas where additional effort are required;
- Withdrawing, leaving a functioning team in place.

As people become confident in the team-working environment, the power of the team develops. People's confidence builds naturally as they begin to see the success of their efforts, as they see the results of their team-work. People often are surprised at their team's effectiveness, as they find solutions to issues and problems that have been worked around or ignored for a long time.

It is clear that there are many different cultures in place in business, industry and the general public and private sectors. Not everyone works in an open environment where ideas and suggestions are welcomed, acknowledged or rewarded. In the more extreme cases, where an autocratic style of management exists, the facilitator must work to protect the newly developing team. They must try to find space for the team to start delivering on its potential by keeping the autocratic manager informed of its development and its efforts – while keeping him or her at a distance. The facilitator also may need to protect the team from over-expectation – where people assume the simple creation of a team will deliver immediate and dramatic results.

The role of the facilitator is a delicate and important one, demanding a high level of inter-personal skills and judgement. A key task for the facilitator is to withdraw from the team, leaving the team with the skill, understanding and ability to be self-sustaining.

Respect

The most important aspect of team-building is both the most obvious and often the most forgotten – respect. It is in how we respect others – their different skills, characteristics and abilities – that we demonstrate true commitment to team-working. Without this fundamental of mutual respect, there is no real prospect of a successful, sustainable team being developed. One must recognise individual contributions as well as contributions to the overall goals and objectives of the business.

TEAM EVOLUTION

Psychologists have studied the dynamics of teams over many years and have identified four clear stages in team evolution:

- Forming;
- Storming;
- Norming;
- Performing.

Forming

A group of people is not a team – however, a group of people brought together with a common objective or task can be brought quickly to form a team.

Once the group is brought together, team dynamics begin to take over. People look to see who else is there, why they have been asked to participate and why others are there or not there, as the case may be.

As the work progresses, in most organisations, a degree of normal business manners is evident. Most groups want to try to be good, to achieve the goals and objectives set for them and there is generally a high level of morale and good spirits. In the autocratic company, however, teams can be slower to form, with people more careful in how they contribute and what they say. People often will wait to see what and how the 'boss' approaches the activity. If the boss is clearly supportive of the effort, and responds positively to the contributions of individuals, then this will lead to a self-reinforcing outcome. If the boss is seen to be negative, then the process is probably doomed to failure or at best a difficult life.

At the first team meeting, the tasks and objectives of the team are introduced and, while they may be agreed as achievable, there is often little sense of ownership of the issues. Depending on the make-up of the team, there may even be some difficulty in them understanding the extent of the problems or the depth of the issues. Usually though, the team members will feel that it is possible to find solutions.

The question of team leadership is often raised. Who should lead the team and how is this person chosen? In most situations in small and medium-sized companies, the leader is self-evident. Where a facilitator is used, then it is usual for the facilitator either to lead the first meeting or to help the manager or chosen team leader to do so. The leader will help the team to focus on its objectives, to allocate specific tasks, to decide when and where team meetings will take place to ensure progress is made and generally to lead the newly-formed team.

Storming

As the name suggests, storming can be a difficult period for the team. By this stage, a number of meetings have taken place and some frustrations may have arisen. Some of the team will be happy with progress to date; others may feel that not enough has been done and that some team members are not committed enough to the tasks. People have come to *care* about the issues and tasks of the team. They have internalised the tasks and taken ownership of them. The team's problems are now *their* problems and they have committed to finding solutions. Team meetings can become quite involved, with forthright discussion and opposing suggestions for solutions being made.

At the same time, team members often can start to compete for position within the team, to move towards leadership positions or to align themselves with others. Quite often, the younger members of the team will lead in terms of levels of energy and enthusiasm and will start to get clear results for their efforts. This, in turn, often can lead to the energising of the more experienced team members.

The leader needs to manage the process carefully now, ensuring that high energy interactions do not degenerate into negativity and that the contributions of all members are recognised. It is also important to encourage all members to contribute. Often the quieter members can be shaded by the more outspoken members, although they may have valuable contributions to make to final solutions. The leader should be able to generate a level of mutual appreciation within the team. It should be clear that individuals have their own skills and attributes and so a level of mutual respect starts to develop.

On the practical side of the team's work, some of the tasks will be yielding to solutions; some will not. It is important to monitor progress and clearly identify which tasks are posing problems. Can the team learn from their successes to help solve the outstanding issues? By focusing attention more clearly on the difficult tasks, the team will move to further develop its problem-solving abilities, to develop its internal capability. An effort needs to be made to come up with potential new ideas for problems, to fully understand the issues and take steps to develop solutions.

Throughout this time, the team leader's role is centrally important. The leader needs to be focused on the big picture. How is the team moving towards its overall goal and objectives? Are all team members contributing? Is the level of commitment and energy to the tasks being shared equally? The leader's role will probably be a mixture of pushing and pulling, cajoling and controlling, bringing on the quieter members of the team and managing the enthusiasm of the young Turks. In some instances, the leader may need to be a conciliator, if confrontation arises.

Norming

By now, the team has become a team. They have developed a sense of respect for each other, recognising their individual contributions to the successes they have achieved. Individuals have come to understand their role within the team and are comfortable with it. The team will move to defend itself against others. Members have a level of interest in the team and its activities and they tend to manage themselves to get on with the tasks set for them and even identify further activities and tasks.

Positive results are being achieved, and the original tasks set for the team have moved well towards completion. Elements that may have caused problems earlier will have been re-examined and alternative solutions suggested until resolutions were identified. The team can discuss issues openly, with a high degree of confidence of positive outcomes.

The team's work, and its achievements, are fully team achievements rather than those of the leader. With this evolution, the role of the leader changes, to being responsible for the further development of capability within the team. They need to help the team understand learning points and opportunities for further growth, as well as recognising achievements and ensuring the team receives recognition for its efforts.

Performing

The team is at the height of its powers. It has developed the ability to solve problems, to address issues in an effective and efficient way.

The original tasks have been completed and the team either has identified more demanding tasks for itself or been allocated other issues by management. People have developed a level of pride in the team and others within the business are aware of it and may want to join.

Discussion within the team often can be robust, but without the negativity of earlier times. Members know that all opinions are expressed from a positive point of view rather than simply to score points off each other. The team is happy to take on extra work and to provide feedback on problems and progress. The team has developed its own shell, with members being protective of the team and its members. Nobody wants to leave.

Further information on the mechanics of team management will be presented in **Chapter 12**.

NEXT STEPS

Now that teams are in place and have identified and addressed a number of key issues or problems facing the business or organisation, possibly following a benchmarking exercise, what other tools should they be armed with?

We now move to look at the other core tools that help to give structure to the teams and help them to tackle objectively the issues and problems identified. Remembering that a core element of the ABC approach is to 'look, see and understand', the next set of core tools will help people 'see the wood for the trees', to progress their capabilities as their skills and experience grow.

So now that we have looked at the basic tools of Lean Service, we will now move on to look at the more advanced tools.

Level 2

Intermediate Lean Service

8: The Work Continues

The fundamentals underpinning Lean Service are about providing a service or making a product: **Quicker, Better, Cheaper … Together**. Often we see that where businesses work quicker, they are also better and consequently are cheaper. The key elements of Lean Service work together to deliver improved performance.

In the previous section, we looked at some basic, fundamentally important tools to help achieve effectiveness and efficiency. By now, people in your business should be comfortable with working in a team, using quality tools such as check sheets and run charts to identify issues and monitor performance and they should have experience looking at the realities of processes.

We now move to the next level of complexity. Many of the techniques presented are natural developments of the tools already presented. Others are new and demand effort to understand them and to use them effectively. The challenge is the same for everyone in the business: how to achieve a sustainable service business in the face of increasing competition. The order in which the tools are used is totally dependent on the business and the priorities identified at any given time.

FACILITATED ASSESSMENT

Note that Facilitated Assessment, rather than Self Assessment, is the appropriate benchmarking approach for companies at this next stage of their development.

The introduction of a trained facilitator into the benchmarking process can greatly increase the level of objectivity. The facilitator will guide the company through the process, ensuring that all questions are fully explained and understood and that the company takes a realistic view of its capabilities and performance.

The facilitated approach can provide a good, simple, effective and secure introduction to international benchmarking. In Europe today, thousands of companies have undergone facilitated benchmarking exercises providing databases of information that is secure, comparable and truly international using the Microscope / Probe and Benchmark Index tools.

9: *Time is Money!*

One of the key measures used in a LB implementation is that of Time, which is critical in a service environment: if your food arrives too late, it may be inedible. Who wants to receive party supplies in the post the day after the party? In a Lean Service environment, you can use time to focus yourself and your staff on just how effectively you are using your time to service your customers, efficiently and well.

Some European benchmarking colleagues who work for the UK's Inland Revenue discovered that, because the post was not opened until mid-day, staff were too late to make up a lodgement before the banks closed each day. This did not seem like a big matter until they realised that it was costing the Inland Revenue several million sterling each year in lost interest. Needless to say, Inland Revenue staff now open the post first thing in the morning, with the appropriate staffing levels in place. Time *is* money!

CHANGE-OVER TIME REDUCTION

In order to process single unit orders, change-over from one job to another must be accomplished with a minimum of fuss, just as one switches from a wordprocessor to a spreadsheet on a PC. However, in an office environment, change-over is often seen as being a time-consuming pain that always loses output due to broken concentration. Thus, it is often easier for staff to carry on with long runs of the same activity rather than dealing with individual items of work as they arrive. "I will finish inputting the invoices into the system before I issue the credit notes". Although this may be convenient for staff, the downside to this approach is that it is demanding of time and invariably leads to long lead times, high levels of backed-up work and, often, to additional costs and lost revenue. In addition, the marketplace increasingly demands greater variety and flexibility, which increases the need to be able to deal with small quantities – even individual orders or requests – as they come in. To meet these demands, set-up times must be reduced to the level where time lost on change-over is negligible.

The task of reducing change-over time can be tackled in the same way as other Lean Service tasks. First, it is essential to know what is actually involved in the change-over before beginning to find ways of improving it. Recording on video what happens during a change-over provides a permanent record, ensuring that all steps in the process are captured.

The fundamentals of reducing change-over times are based on the identification of *internal* and *external* tasks (see **Figure 9.1**):

- **Internal tasks:** Tasks that can only be performed when the process is stopped – changing from one system to another, attending to colleagues' requests, etc.

- **External tasks:** Tasks that can be performed while the process is still running – getting ready, locating paperwork, having sufficient supplies, etc.

Once what happens during the change-over has been recorded, the set-up improvement team can identify wastes and areas for improvement. The use of standardised processes, standardised forms, standardised methods and many other points of detail can have a significant impact in reducing overall set-up time. Industry journals and sales brochures for the latest processes often can be used to help the team see new ways of achieving their objective.

When a better, shorter and simpler way of performing the set-up has been arrived at, record it. Train all relevant staff on the new way of working and ensure that this approach is followed – all the time.

FIGURE 9.1: CHANGE-OVER TIME

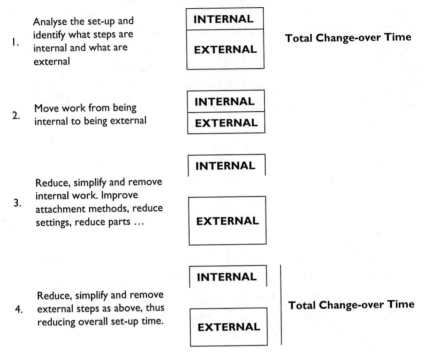

But remember, the quickest and best change-over – and the easiest to perform – is the set-up that is not done. If process design can remove the need for a change of system, then it is not necessary to change-over from using another system. If planning can plan efficiently, and sales can sell a relatively standardised service, then the need for change-overs is minimised.

REDUCING BATCH SIZES

Another key feature of Lean Service is the drive to reduce batch sizes. If you build up large batches of work in front of your staff, then it will take them a long time to clear the backlog and to be able to respond to customers in real-time. The optimum batch size is one unit, to ensure that no delays are encountered in a process and that no WIP builds up.

Imagine a three-step process with five items to process, as shown in **Figure 9.2**. In a batch processing system (order entry, for example), all items must be processed in area 1 before they can move to area 2, and all items must be processed in area 2 before moving to area 3. In a single item system, once a unit is processed in area A, it can be worked on in area B and, once completed there, it can be worked on in area C. If the processing time for each area for each unit is one minute, how long it will take to produce five items from each process?

FIGURE 9.2: BATCH VS SINGLE ITEM PROCESSING

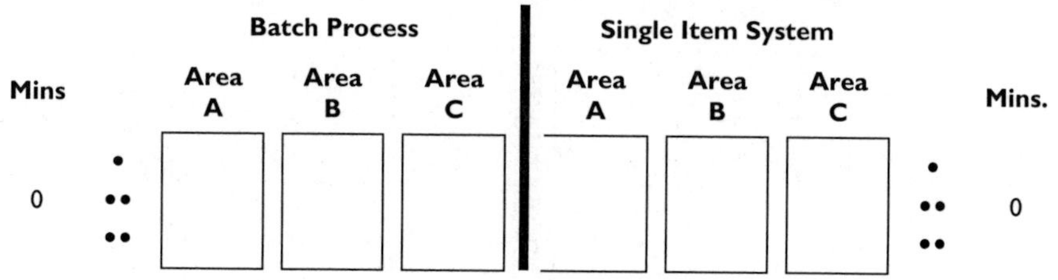

Take the time to work this out. Then check your solution against **Figure 9.3**.

It is clear that a single item system needs very much less time to complete the work than the batch processing system. In addition, less WIP is created.

If the process is stepped up to a continuous system, major differences in WIP levels will be seen. This equates to cash, as jobs not completed cannot be billed to a client.

Most importantly, the time required in a continuous system for processing – paperwork, for example – is half that of a batch processing system. A single item system is the ideal – however, practical considerations may make this impossible to achieve today. But the same basic argument holds if batch size can be reduced from 100 units to 50, or 50 units to 20, or 20 units to 10 – the closer you can get to single item / continuous processing, the bigger the savings.

FIGURE 9.3: BATCH VS SINGLE ITEM PROCESSING - DEVELOPED

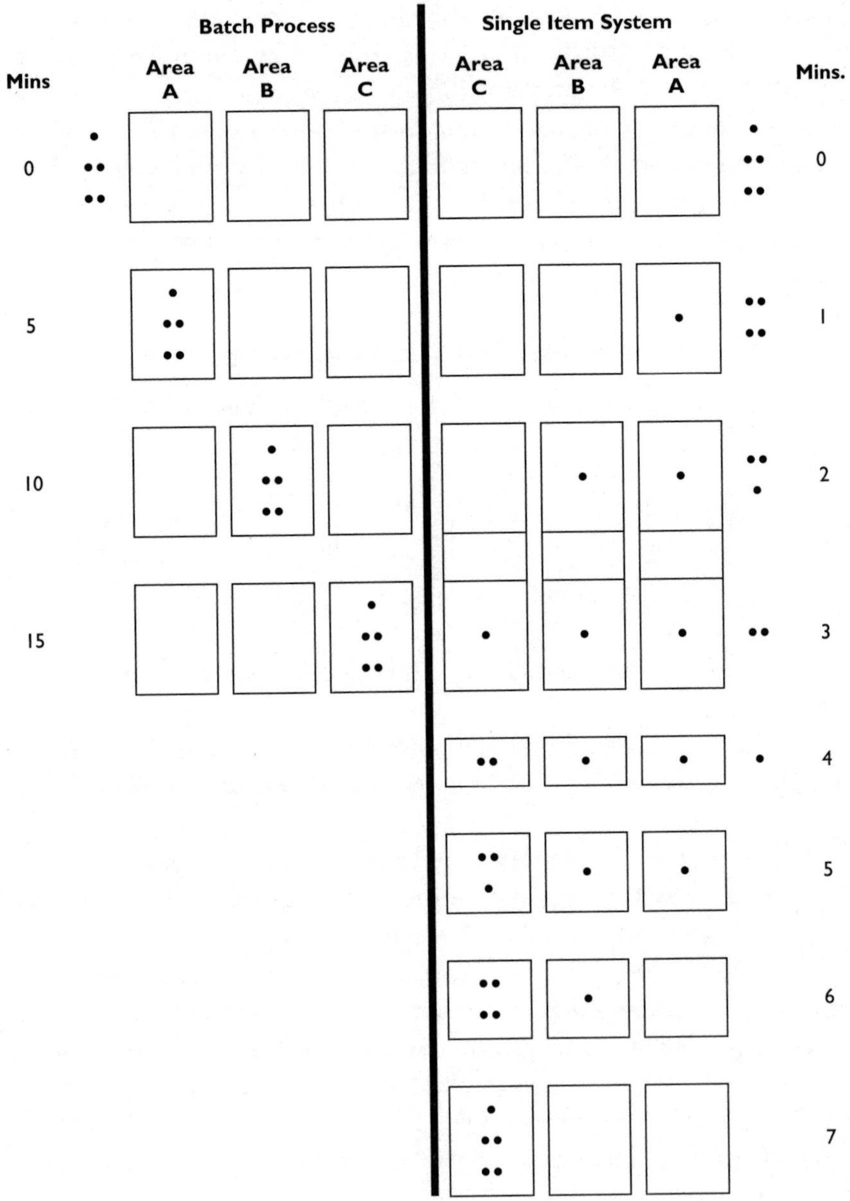

THE SHADOW SYSTEM

The most costly piece of paper in any operation is the one that cannot be found when needed! The time lost due to missing paperwork often can greatly outweigh the cost of the tools themselves. How often have you spent time looking for a specific piece of paper, or a stapler, a disc, a file or even a working pen?

The shadow system was developed to help address the issue of missing or mislaid equipment. The first step in developing the shadow system is to define what you actually need to have available to you to get your job done. The focus here is usually on the ancillary equipment such as staplers, staples, pens, highlighters, spare documents, phone books and the like rather than a computer or telephone. Once the list is made of what is needed to get the job done, then comes making a space in the work area, with the outline of required items or an identification mark inscribed on the board. If the item is missing, it is clear to see and also easy to know which one is missing. **Figure 9.4** shows two ways of keeping items in a service area.

FIGURE 9.4: TOOLBOX VS SHADOW BOARD

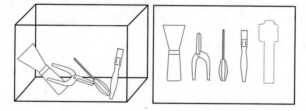

What tool is missing from the toolbox? What tool is missing from the shadow board? Which way of keeping tools would you prefer to rely on?

The simple fact of having defined locations for equipment and supplies can help to reduce lost time spent looking for missing items. Many of our desks have dedicated trays in our drawers but they seldom designate what should be in each compartment and so they collect clutter, which delays us finding the item we need when we need it.

The system can be extended to handle files, where multiple people have access to individual files. In this system, each worker can have identifying tags, usually colour-coded, with each person having perhaps three tags of the one colour. If they remove a file from the central cabinet, they leave one of their tags in the cabinet in place of the file they have taken, showing their colleagues who has the file. If someone else needs the file, they know immediately who has it and can ask whether the file is now free to be accessed. This is a simple system that can save a lot of time when it comes to searching for shared files.

EARLY WARNING SYSTEMS

Many of the tools covered so far, such as check sheets and run charts, tell you about what has happened in the past. Now let's look at LB techniques that will tell you about the future, giving early warning of problems that could lead to failures, rejects or lost sales arising in the future.

For example, modern photocopiers can warn of the completion of a batch, alerting the operator to the need to remove a print job and change-over to the next job. In addition, the system can alert the operator to a machine stoppage, calling them to free the machine and restart printing. Most modern photocopiers and printers also will let you know:

- When the paper has run out;
- When the toner is about to run out;
- When the colour cartridges are approaching the end of their capacity;
- When the feeders are jammed;
- Which feeder element is jammed;
- When the machine needs a service.

For the technician, there are many more pieces of information that the current machines can advise them of, to help them ensure that your printer / copier is working at its best and that it will be available to you to do your work as and when you need to do it ... provided that you take heed of the warning signals and address the needs of the machine.

The key objective of using these early warning devices is to free staff to do other, more value-adding (and usually, more interesting) work. There are some other uses for such systems that can make life easier and more comfortable. A system of level gauges and warning lights can be used to capture the level of oil in a heating tank, ensuring that the heating oil does not run out at the wrong time. If the level can be detected as being low, it can be refilled. But, if the tank runs out, then the hassle and cost of getting the system refilled and the boiler restarted can be frustrating and costly – and meanwhile staff go cold, or worse, go home!

Mark Your Gauges!

Another simple technique to help ensure that plant and machinery operate correctly is to mark gauges.

Fuel, temperature, or oil gauges in a car indicate clearly what areas are good and what areas are bad – red is usually a sign of a danger zone. You can apply a similar approach to service industry. If displays are marked, the operator can see immediately whether the needles are pointing to the right zone. If there are multiple gauges in a control panel, why not align all the correct operating zones so that an operator can see immediately whether any dial indicates outside the normal range. This idea comes from the air line industry where basic systems are used to help the service provider – the pilot – to do their jobs without having to more work than is necessary, reducing risk and improving the chance for the service, your safe flight, to be delivered effectively and efficiently.

The same approach can be applied to machine settings. By noting settings on the machine in the relevant positions, staff can know what settings need to be. As an example, think of a postage franking machine. If the instructions are kept close by, then credit can be uploaded and basic supplies can be available in a timely way.

Many service centres use visual displays (instead of a complaints book) to show the level, number and type of calls being recorded as issues from their customers. By clearly identifying the issues, say by using colour-coding, staff can quickly identify critical customers and critical issues. Without some form of 'prioritising', key issues and key customers can 'get lost' in the volume of issues being addressed, leading to poor customer service.

One of the big challenges facing business today is the speed of change in the marketplace. If you take too long to fix problems in your service offering, it is quite likely that someone else will have developed your idea, brought it to market and maybe even that the market will have moved on. Speed of response is essential to achieve success.

10: Operations Control Systems

Three basic forms of operations control system are used in companies employing Lean practices:

- Produce to order;
- Kanban;
- Rate-based scheduling.

You know these systems in your daily life. At a restaurant, you believe they are 'producing to order' what you ask for when you ask for it. Much work is done in preparation beforehand, but usually the meal is produced as required.

The Kanban system is what is often known as a two bin system. Imagine you like coffee and don't like to be without a cup of instant coffee before you go to work. By having two jars of coffee at home – one being used and the other in reserve, for when the first jar runs out – you can ensure that you will always have coffee when you want it, without having to go to the shops to buy it when the first jar has run out. This is in effect a 'two bin system' or kanban system.

The third system is more basic and is at the foundation of much of our lives. A rate-based scheduling system looks at the usage of a service or utility over time and moves to make the service or utility available based on an analysis of the usage patterns. The electricity that powers our homes operates as a rate-based system. The energy providers produce electricity based on the analysed needs of our economy, with a little in reserve, just in case.

The type of system chosen for any given service is usually selected based on the history of use of the service and its likely future (see **Figure 10.1**).

FIGURE 10.1: OPERATIONS CONTROL SYSTEMS

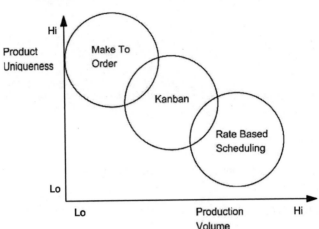

PRODUCE TO ORDER

If the service or product is fairly unique or is required in low volumes, then a produce to order (PTO) approach is probably most appropriate.

As the name suggests, the service or product is produced only when an order is received. Very little, if any, stock of finished goods is held, because it could become obsolete or have the wrong configuration by the time a customer places an order. Imagine a fast food restaurant, keeping lots of burgers ready for sale – customers are usually much happier ordering a fresh meal rather than taking one that has been under the warming lights for the last 10 or 15 minutes.

Nonetheless, many processes can be delivered more quickly by doing some preparation work in advance. Say, by having documents ready for order entry rather than having to think what information is required each and every time you go to take an order. Or having food partly prepared in advance, or having some face towels warming gently in a barber's shop, or the right equipment on a pre-sterilised tray for a surgeon. Little things can make a big difference in reducing the overall time to deliver a service, if we can prepare early. The old adage 'Time is money' is still true, and customers today are more likely to want their service delivered quickly and well rather than wait for it. Time can be a major factor of competition.

The PTO system is the ultimate goal of all Lean operations. Why would a business want to target anything less? In a PTO business, stocks are at a minimum, response time is very short and flexibility is high. The real art in a PTO system is to be able to achieve the benefits of mass production (rate-based scheduling) while providing the customer with the option of mass customisation.

THE KANBAN TWO BIN SYSTEM

The Kanban or two bin system is suited to medium-volume, medium-diversity items. One of the simplest examples of the two bin system can be found in most offices, where usually extra paper is kept beside the photocopier so that it doesn't run out.

The system is very simple to implement. An estimate of the requirement is made, usually based on history and forecasts. This volume then defines the size of the Kanban or bin. If the volume to be produced is chosen as half a week's supply, then two bins are prepared, each capable of holding half a week's requirement. Product is drawn from the first bin until it is empty, at which time the second bin is accessed and the empty bin is replenished.

The bin can be replenished from a local storage area, central stores or by a supplier. An empty bin is the trigger for replenishment. There is no checking necessary to count balance stocks or to check stores. As the operation of the system becomes ingrained in the business, and suppliers become more assured with the process of replenishment, it is possible to reduce the stock held in each bin.

And, from the previous chapter, you can see the possibility of using the two bin system for your photocopier: not just keeping a stock of paper but adding a spare toner cartridge to your two bin system to make sure that you do not run out of any of these either.

Note that the term bin is used loosely: 'bins' can be bins, drums, pallets, bags or even silos depending on the material itself. At home, we use a two bin system for cocoa ...

RATE-BASED SCHEDULING

The rate-based scheduling (RBS) approach is best suited to mature services with secure positions in the market, where history and forecasts indicate that market demand is steady and the service lends itself to steady state, dedicated delivery. If you know the demands for a given service from the market, then it becomes possible to staff accordingly based on the demands of the market.

Under RBS, time, staff and resources are allocated based on rolling forecasts. Call centres are an example where staff are recruited to service major market campaigns or at specific times when demand is strong for the service.

As volumes increase, there is an opportunity to move towards more dedicated, automated systems, where the effort required to automate processes can be recouped over the life of the system. Many companies now use automated answering systems to help them to reduce the cost of administrative staff answering telephones. The use of dedicated web-based FAQs (Frequently Asked Questions) is another example, as are the semi-expert systems increasingly used to troubleshoot computer systems.

Note that the type of system best suited to the provision of a given service can – and often will – change over the life cycle of the service (see **Figure 10.2**).

FIGURE 10.2: LIFE CYCLE AND CHOICE OF DELIVERY SYSTEMS

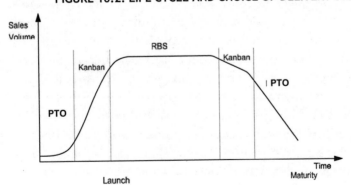

Imagine the launch of a new online service. Because it is new to the market, it is unlikely that there will be immediate significant demand from the market. In this instance, a PTO system may be most appropriate. As the market becomes aware of the product, then it may be time to move towards a system where some key elements of the service can be pre-prepared and held at the ready for quick deployment. Once the service has been accepted by the market, it probably makes sense to automate some of the delivery of the service, investing in infrastructure to support the service. Alternatively, dedicated teams can be allocated to support the service in the field. As the service demand falls off, the appropriate operations system will most likely reverse as demand falls off.

MAINTENANCE

How can you expect machines or processes to produce high quality goods as required, if the machinery is not maintained properly?

The Service Maintenance (SM) concept takes the pragmatic approach that, to provide good services, you need to be able to rely on your equipment and systems. When you start a job, you want to be able to finish it, without having to fix a machine during the job. Staff should be trained in the basics of maintenance, to know the standard operating conditions of the machine and also to recognise when something is going wrong.

Remember when you rode a bicycle? It was usually easier to tighten the chain before it fell off and jammed the sprocket than to ignore it, release and fix it and then tighten it *after* it jammed. The same rule applies in business: if a problem is caught before it jams a system, it is generally easier to address.

By using the SM approach, leading companies are not only 'addressing before jams' but are also developing systems and processes to the point where they will not jam. This effort has resulted in major benefits. Much of the effort required to achieve this is basic, using well-proven ideas and concepts.

Systems and machines break down. To prevent this, they need to be maintained. If they break down when they are needed for delivering a job, this can cause real problems. Maintenance, when correctly used, can improve the overall performance of a piece of important equipment.

Much maintenance activity is based on the understanding of machine life cycles, represented in **Figure 10.3**.

FIGURE 10.3: THE PROBABILITY OF FAILURE

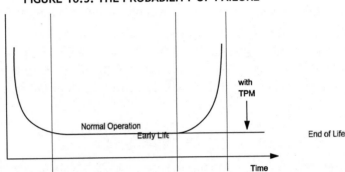

Engineers have identified that all systems and machines have a life cycle. The early days of their working lives are likely to give rise to teething problems. Once a machine has passed through this phase, it tends to work normally for a long period but, as it approaches the end of its working life, it tends to give problems again. The work of maintenance is to extend the good working time for the machine so that you can get your work done using the least effort.

The Basics of Maintenance

Maintenance makes an effort to prolong the period of normal operation.

The basics of good maintenance can be described quite simply:

- Work areas need to be organised, clean and free of clutter;
- Good housekeeping should be the norm;
- Staff need to care for their machines;
- Staff need to understand the process;
- Staff should do basic checks on the machines;
- Operators should do basic maintenance on the machines.

Cleaning

By cleaning their working area, staff develop a sense of ownership for their environment. This mundane task also gives staff a chance to get to know their equipment better and to be able to identify problems as they develop. As staff become more experienced, they will build on their ability to predict failures and problems before these become sources of loss for the business.

A clean workplace is generally a better and nicer environment to work in. A clean work area is also generally a safer work area. If clutter is removed, and material and equipment are correctly organized, then trip hazards are minimised. It seems obvious, but good housekeeping can help a great deal in presenting your business well and in building the morale of people throughout the organisation. A clean desk policy, where work areas are kept tidy, not only can contribute to a better working environment but also can contribute to more efficient work as less time is spent looking for documents, information or files.

Organising

The old adage 'a place for everything and everything in its place' is very appropriate here. Time spent looking for a missing file or document is often time that could have been spent more productively.

There should be specific locations defined for consumable materials, files, collateral and office equipment that is used occasionally. Machine-specific consumables should be located beside the machine, preferably on a shadow system. Effective shelving systems can be used to organise items in an appropriate fashion, saving time and ensuring that you don't run out of necessary items at a critical time.

Areas for consumable materials and collateral goods can help ensure that sufficient materials are available for the operation, but not too much.

An organised work area is more effective and efficient than a disorganised one.

Caring

People need to care for their systems and machines, their work areas and their work. Managers need to care about their processes.

It may seem strange to use 'care' in a business sense, but it is a valid use of the word. Unless you care about what you are doing, you are being 'careless' with your work. You have had experiences of service interactions where it seemed to you that the service provider did not 'care' about you, the customer. These tend to be negative experiences.

If a photocopier, printer or server stops, people need to care enough to get it going again, quickly and correctly. People need to care enough about what they are doing to want to work to improve performance, to want to use the LB tools to identify root causes of problems.

Understanding

Operators need to be trained to understand their systems, their processes and the impact of changes they might make. People often *think* they know what they are doing and managers can easily *assume* that operators understand the detailed impact of their actions. But this is often not true. It is not enough that the manager, supervisor or team lead understands the process; businesses that want to be Lean must work to the point where all key staff know and understand the processes they work with and are committed to improving things.

Fixed Time Maintenance

As the name implies, this maintenance takes place based on time. Daily, weekly, monthly or yearly checks, adjustments and replacements are made, to ensure that machines perform at their optimum. Parts are changed before they reach the end of their service life. By doing this, there is a high probability that the machine will operate faultlessly between services. The time between changing components and parts is based on design information and experience. The system is best known in the automotive world where oil, filters and plugs are changed according to time or mileage criteria.

In business, it is often difficult to assemble sufficient data to know when parts are approaching the end of their service lives – this can mean that some parts are replaced before it is necessary. The more complex the machine, the harder it is to be accurate in replacement schedules.

Condition-based Maintenance

By monitoring changes in plant and equipment, it is possible to notice deterioration and plan a response before failure occurs.

Many of the actions used to implement condition-based maintenance (CBM) are simple:

- Wiping a surface;
- Listening to a machine: is the copier 'grinding'?
- Smelling for heat build-up;
- Looking at a machine action;
- Feeling for vibrations.

Obviously, care needs to be taken to avoid injury when using these techniques but they can be very effective in the early diagnosis of developing machine problems. Staff can develop a very heightened sense of their equipment and often can detect a deteriorating condition before it fails. They may not always be able to describe technically what is going wrong but they can often help the 'fixer' to hone in on the issue.

Case Study 2: Control Rooms at Irish Rail

Iarnród Éireann - Irish Rail is the State-owned railway in Ireland and a division of the CIE semi-State transport company. The organisation is the provider of all rail services in Ireland, including the cross-border service to Belfast, and owns and maintains all rolling stock in-house. Since 2000, more than €1bn has been invested in new rolling stock to modernise the national fleet. This required a major change in the way trains are maintained and overhauled. In 2007, faced with declining Government subvention and a need to significantly improve efficiency and reduce costs, the Engineering department introduced a change management programme based on the introduction of LEAN principles. This centred on the training of engineering staff in LEAN tools and processes and their application in the daily business. After initial external support was removed, the processes and use of LEAN tools is now an everyday norm supporting the maintenance and overhaul of the Irish Rail rolling stock fleet. Without doubt, the most successful LEAN tool used to date has been the implementation of location-specific control rooms.

Each location throughout the business – such as a maintenance, overhaul or manufacturing facility – has a basic control room. Simple visualisation techniques are used to display the key metrics required to show the overall performance and the current business status for that location. Deviations from planned output and barriers or issues are clearly shown and necessary corrective actions with clear ownership assigned.

A standard format control room meeting takes place at least once a day in each control room. The meetings are short – typically, 15 minutes – and involve all stakeholders necessary to deliver the business output for that location, including any external contractors. Issues are raised, actioned, ownership assigned and addressed and progress reported on during the meeting as required. Wall-mounted magnetic surface whiteboards are used to record and display all information, with each subject (for example, planned output, performance or material) allocated its own whiteboard. Each whiteboard has an owner, who presents the key information from their whiteboard at the control room meeting. At the end, everybody leaves on the same understanding of the current business state – they know what we should have done, what we did, what we need to do and actions required to address barriers to this.

The control room is a focal point of each location and is the key to managing our maintenance-centred business. When asked what change has made the biggest impact over the last seven years, Engineering staff point to the control room. Since 2008, implementing LEAN has delivered an improvement in Engineering performance of 75%, while reducing costs by 30%, with 20% less headcount. The control Room is a key part of this success.

11: *Practical Quality*

Quality is a universal concern for all businesses and organisations. It is equally important for public bodies that provide services to companies and individuals, as it is for private sector companies.

An understanding of quality and quality tools is essential to build competitiveness into the future. Customers and clients will not accept the levels of quality that were acceptable even 10 years ago. The old attitude of 'it will be good enough!' must be destroyed and replaced with one where products and services are always of the highest quality, and worth the asking price.

Ireland has been a world leader in the adoption of the ISO 9000 quality standard. This has had both a positive and a negative effect on Irish business. On the positive side, the adoption of the standard has meant that the business takes quality seriously and has appointed a quality champion or representative. On the negative side, many people seemed to think that, once an ISO 9000 system is in place, 'quality' has been taken care of. If there is a 'Quality Department', surely quality is their responsibility. However, **Quality is Everybody's Responsibility!** Quality cannot be added after the fact. No amount of measuring, testing, counting or evaluating will add quality to a service or product. Quality can only be added to a service or product during the value-adding parts of the process.

Consider a typical service organisation, say a bank. If the bank is cluttered, disorganised and badly-run with bad-mannered staff or overly-complicated systems, people will think poorly of the place and wonder whether their money is better elsewhere. Restaurant customers who find the toilets dirty or badly taken care of can only hope the kitchens are better managed and more hygienic.

People throughout the business need to understand that they are an integral part of this quality chain and not separate from it.

This shared awareness of quality and how employees are a part of, and integrated into, the quality chain needs to be introduced to all employees by a committed and dedicated management. True business excellence and customer care are at the heart of this approach. Training of management and staff becomes an essential part of getting this message across, until it becomes the natural way of life within the business.

The approach could be called 'quality function deployment' for small and medium-sized companies. By deploying quality throughout the business, by making everyone responsible for their own contribution to quality, real levels of improvement can be achieved. The approach is akin to expecting that all employees act with skill and dedication – like craftsmen of old. People need to care about what they do if they are to have respect for themselves, their output and the business.

But how do you translate these high ideals into practical reality? There are many books written on the detail of quality systems. For a very deep understanding of the theory of quality, these texts should be studied. If a practical and immediate move to improve operational performance is required, there is a core of tools that can help do this, easily. You have already been introduced to the core LB tools of physical flow and process flow analysis, check sheets and run charts, all supported by the use of teams. Now let's look at some further, relatively simple, quality tools and techniques that can help to identify the root sources of waste in an operation and to address them.

LB OR ISO – WHICH COMES FIRST?

The question is often asked, which comes first, the ISO quality standard or a LB initiative? The answer is that it depends. The new version of ISO 9000 now includes continuous improvement as an integral part of the quality system. The new system even says that businesses should benchmark themselves. So now the distance between ISO and LB has closed.

By taking the LB route, a business will strengthen the abilities and capabilities of its staff, while developing and improving its processes and performance. By following the route outlined in this book, including objective benchmarking against international sectoral performance and practice models, a business truly will be working towards developing its capabilities. When this basic work of improving and developing internal performance is completed, it should be a relatively simple matter to create procedures for the processes, and to write the manual to ISO standards.

If, on the other hand, the time and resources are available from the beginning to follow the ISO implementation route, then the business undoubtedly will succeed in writing procedures to describe their processes and, in time, will improve those processes when it adopts continuous improvement and benchmarking techniques.

Both routes will lead to a similar goal, although the ABC route is most likely to get there earlier and with a more company-wide team-based approach. The ABC organisation will have built the capability of its people in improving systems and processes and in working together. The ISO organisation will be very good at writing procedures and building a quality manual. Commitment to the goal of improving the business operations is the key, either way. You pay your money and take your choice!

CUSTOMER COMPLAINTS AS A DATA SOURCE

All businesses have customers or clients, whether they be public or private enterprises, service or manufacturing operations, profit or non-profit. The fact that customers or clients exist usually means that there will be a high degree of customer satisfaction, but equally it means that there may be some level of customer dissatisfaction or complaint also.

Customer complaints are a very rich source of opportunity to improve processes. However, it is important to realise that not all customer complaints are valid or true. This is often a delicate issue, but needs to be recognised and managed. If a business or organisation accepts a totally customer-biased response to complaints, then it is open to abuse by a small percentage of its clients.

That said, the first question a business or organisation needs to ask itself here is: 'Are records available of all complaints received?'. If there is no system to capture complaints received, then it is unlikely that complaints will be captured, and even more unlikely that they will be analysed and less unlikely again that the business will benefit from the potential to improve its processes that such complaints could deliver to the business.

A system to capture customer complaints can be as simple as a file to store written complaints and a simple form to capture telephoned or spoken complaints.

Use a check sheet to analyse the complaints. Many companies often deal with individual complaints as just that – individual complaints. They fail to analyse complaints over time, and thus miss trends, or seasonal factors, or hot spots in their processes that contribute to complaints.

An action team should be formed to analyse and discuss the complaints in an effort to devise a company-wide response to the issues identified by the analysis. Often complaints are handled by sales or quality department staff, without recourse to the sections of the business responsible for the source of the problem.

Then use a run chart to record:

- The overall level of customer complaints;
- The causes of complaints.

The run chart gives the business the opportunity to monitor progress over time and to work to reduce the overall incidence of complaints.

A customer complaints team that is representative of all elements of the operation can lead to a highly focused and successful initiative across the business.

THE MEASLES DIAGRAM

Much modern service business is complex and often of quite a large scale. The measles diagram helps to identify areas of such processes that cause problems. It is an evolution from the check sheet where, rather than working with a list of problems that may occur in a process, a pictogram of the process is developed. Each time a problem occurs in a particular part of the process, a dot – a 'measle' – is placed on the pictogram (see **Figure 11.1**). Examples of this can be seen in the control rooms of large scale service providers, where hot spots can be identified by the number of spots or the graphically-represented traffic activity at specific points on the process. Telecoms service providers have means of identifying nodal traffic congestion, electricity and other utility service providers have similar graphical systems to allow their system operators to identify potential critical points and to take steps to remedy or alleviate any issues arising.

FIGURE 11.1: THE MEASLES DIAGRAM

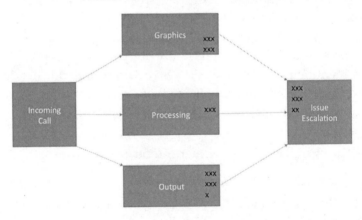

The level of detail of the pictogram depends on an estimate of where problems are occurring. If more detail is needed, it is often better to draw detailed sketches of specific parts of a process and leave them located at different points in the process rather than developing one big sketch for the whole process.

HISTOGRAMS

Histograms allow you to 'see' data using a graphical approach.

Information is gathered from the process and represented using a bar graph. The histogram is usually used to represent frequency of occurrence of data. It can be used successfully to record such diverse data sets as sales of trucks by model, to numbers of customers at different times of day, to numbers of faults or complaints recorded by department.

The use of the histogram in a sales environment can be greatly enhanced by the introduction of a target line. In the following example, the sales of different models of trucks are used to show how the histogram can be used (**Figure 11.2**).

FIGURE 11.2: SALES OF TRUCKS - DATA

Week No:	10				
Model	"45"	"75"	"95"	"6x4"	"8x4"
Number Sold	3	7	4	2	3
Target	2	8	3	3	2

The data is usually captured daily or weekly to give managers an insight into the trends at play. The data is then entered onto the histogram.

FIGURE 11.3: SALES OF TRUCKS - HISTOGRAM

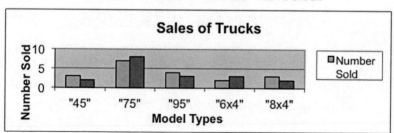

The inclusion of the target line on the histogram for sales can be helpful as both a challenge – and a recognition of achievement.

Another use of the histogram is to check variation in a process. In this next example, the number of customers coming into a shop is measured, as in **Figure 11.4**.

FIGURE 11.4: CUSTOMERS AT DIFFERENT TIMES OF THE DAY - DATA

Time of Day	9-10	10-11	11-12	12-1	1-2	2-3	3-4	4-5	5-6
Number	13	46	38	73	86	45	31	47	80

Now the histogram is developed further to help you to see the data, as in **Figure 11.5**.

FIGURE 11.5: CUSTOMERS AT DIFFERENT TIMES OF THE DAY - HISTOGRAM

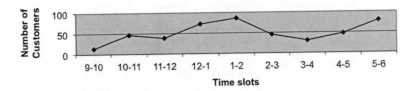

If the data shows when customers are most likely to come in, then it becomes possible to staff accordingly, improving both customer service and staff engagement. The histogram can be helpful in seeing these results and initiating action to resolve them.

CONTROLLING PROCESSES

The control of processes is essential to delivering quality services to customers. A number of techniques have been developed to help management to gain, and to retain, confidence that procedures will be followed and quality standards maintained.

Starting Up

Before a process can be 'released to customers', it needs to be started. For example, airline pilots work through extensive checklists before taking to the air. In a more mundane business, think of a fast-food outlet where controls and checklists are in place to ensure refrigeration, cooking and maintenance temperatures are correct before the first meals of the day are served.

In a front-office business, are all the correct forms and documents in place, and in sufficient quantities, before opening for business? In a retail outlet, have shelves been restocked, are bags available in place, are sufficient till rolls in place and is the shop tidy? Most business can benefit from having a 'pre-opening' or pre-starting business checklist to ensure that all relevant items are present and correct.

If there are new promotions, new procedures or new staff, staff can be prepared and ready to deal with any changes to the norm.

Getting Ready Control Sheet

A 'getting ready' quality check often will include such details as checking that the correct equipment and instructions are available and that key operational parameters are being achieved, such as checking the temperature of ovens, the flow rate of air in an operating theatre, or the level of gas pressure in a pub cellar. An example of a getting ready control sheet is presented in **Figure 11.6**.

FIGURE 11.6: GETTING READY CONTROL SHEET

Staff Member:		
Date:		
Shelves stocked		Checked
	Dairy	
	Veg	
	Meat	
	Dry Goods	
Tills Ready		
	Rolls	
	Bags	
Promotions		
1		
2		

The use of simple-to-use, and easily developed getting ready control sheets can help ensure that, once a job has been started, it can be delivered through to conclusion without unduly rushing around looking for items. This can bring major benefits, in terms of ultimate service quality at low cost.

Running Your Process

Once the process is started correctly, it is important to keep it running and to be sure that it is running at the quality levels set. Since the manager cannot be present all the time to ensure this, in process inspection (IPI) is a means of ensuring quality levels are maintained. Examples of IPI include public toilets, where a control sheet shows who last performed a check on cleanliness – and when. In major food outlets, regular checks are made on the temperature of chilled food cabinets. In power generation stations, regular checks are made on the status of many parameters to ensure that the plant is running both efficiently and well.

Run charts can record IPI data and monitor the process. Run charts can help staff see whether a process is running well or badly, helping them to decide whether and when they need to intervene to make a difference. An example of a run chart is presented in **Figure 11.7**.

FIGURE 11.7: RUN CHART

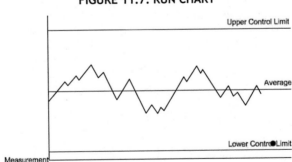

Sampling Your Process

The process has been started and the normal checks and controls are in place, but is management *really* getting a full and accurate view?

In a service business, blind testing provides the opportunity of seeing what the customer perceives. This can be done by telephoning the business or by getting a friend or specialist analysis company to obtain service from the business, to see just what the experience is like for customers or clients. You are probably familiar with process sampling through the work of critics in the newspapers and blogs on-line. Individuals whose opinions are respected can give us a good guide as to what we can expect from a particular service. The development on on-line customer feedback systems such as TripAdvisor can give this 'critic' status to an even broader range of individuals, possibly adding to your appreciation of what you are planning on receiving!

In all these cases, you need to be aware of what is actually being sampled. Are the attributes readily identified and identifiable? Are the variables too many so that they cloud the judgment process? Are the attributes that the critic appreciates the same ones that you agree with – and do you value them equally?

In a service business, the question of what to measure often can be a difficult one. Normal in process inspection can measure only two or three attributes at a time. However, most services have many more attributes. The sample analysis report facilitates this process. By restricting the analysis to a small part of the service, it becomes possible to check and measure many more attributes than during the normal IPI. It is therefore important to identify which part of the overall service is seen by the customer as being a key element that decides their service experience. An example of the sample analysis report is presented in **Figure 11.8**.

FIGURE 11.8: SAMPLE ANALYSIS REPORT

	Sample				
	1	2	3	4	5
Weight					
Colour					
Texture					
Temperature					
Taste					
Presentation					
Smell					

CUSTOMER COMPLAINT REPORTS

Your customer complaints can be seen as an invaluable source of information for management and staff focused on an improvement initiative. Since the complaints represent waste, careful analysis may provide insights into the causes of poor customer experience. The breakdown of complaints into categories can help focus attention on the relevant area. An example of a customer complaints report is presented in **Figure 11.9**.

FIGURE 11.9: CUSTOMER COMPLAINTS REPORT

Complaint No.	Description	Fault	Disposition
407	Software still not working	Customer had not entered password correctly	Fixed, need to improve instructions
408	Computer won't work	Not turned on	Instructions not clear
409	Computer won't work	Faulty battery	Discuss with supplier

The Customer Complaint report can provide a basis for feedback to staff and managers. By quantifying objectively the source of faults, factual information to discuss with your team is gained.

OUTPUT REPORTS

Output reports can be used in many different areas of a service operation. They provide management, and staff, with the opportunity to capture information, typically from individual areas of an operation, sections or employees. The reports can be used in very many ways to show the real performance of an operation.

In many cases, the use of the data can be helpful in identifying systemic issues rather than staff-related issues. An 'output report' can be a very effective 'voice' for staff as they try to identify issues affecting their ability to deliver a good service to the customers. The output reports can be relatively simple, as in **Figure 11.10**, an example of a sales report.

FIGURE 11.10: OUTPUT REPORT 1 - SALES

Day	
Shift	
Sales €	

All the information that the manager gets is the overall output for the shift. This information could be charted, using a run chart, to see whether it varies over time. However, the information is quite limited.

Developing the report a stage further, you could look for records of the amount of lost time being incurred during a shift. Was the cash register not working, were there no bags, was the credit card machine 'acting up' (again?), was there something that stopped people doing the job they were paid to do? This could lead to a report as in **Figure 11.11**.

The manager and staff members now both have a view of trends over time and can begin to discuss improvement initiatives to address downtime.

FIGURE 11.11: OUTPUT REPORT 2 - SALES

Day	
Shift	
Sales €	
Lost Time hrs	

The next evolution of the output report provides further information to manager and staff member and can be very helpful in identifying issues, as in **Figure 11.12**.

FIGURE 11.12: OUTPUT REPORT 3 - SALES

Time	9-10	10-11	11-12	12-13	13-14	14-15	15-16	16-17
Day								
Shift								
Sales €								
Lost Time hrs								

This level of detail lends itself to further analysis, with the run chart format being particularly suited to this work. As an example, **Figure 11.13** presents the data from a typical process over an eight-hour working day.

FIGURE 11.13: OUTPUT CHART

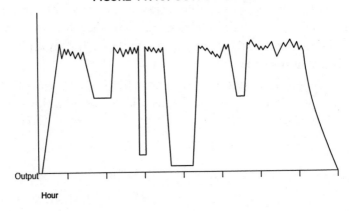

Examining this run chart may identify issues that may have been neglected or missed over time, as in **Figure 11.14**.

FIGURE 11.14: OUTPUT CHART - ANNOTATED

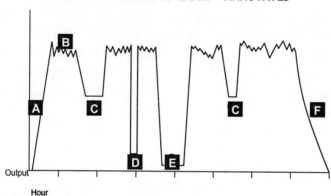

The issues identifiable in **Figure 11.14** include:

A: Start-up losses: Time can be lost first thing in the morning, getting materials organised and systems started. Could this waste be reduced by employing a 'start-up person' who comes in early to prepare rather than losing the output of the full work force?

B: 'Normal' operations: Customers calling, with a small degree of variations. These variations often can be difficult to address or may even be completely random, but they can be very fertile ground for improvement and suggestion activities for the team to try and find ways to increase the level of customer engagement;

C: Coffee break: Half the staff at a time, meaning a reduction in the number of people on the system and a fall-off in the number of transactions completed during that time;

D: System crash / breakdown: Requires an input from maintenance to get the process running again;

E: Lunch break and afternoon tea!

F: Closing down losses: As people get ready to go home, they begin to wind down and clean up.

The chart can be used to record the timing and level of incoming telephone calls, thereby identifying an optimised pattern of attendance for reception and order-taking staff, ensuring sufficient staff are present when clients require service.

But there is one loss not shown on this run chart that is often missed: the difference between system design output levels and normal operating levels, as shown in **Figure 11.15**. Often processes are run below their design levels due to poor standards, unclear expectations, poor infrastructure, maintenance or support. You should try to run processes at their design speeds and even beyond, by fixing the issues that normally prevent you from doing this.

FIGURE 11.15: OUTPUT CHART SHOWING POTENTIAL

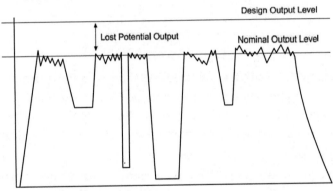

Output reports and charts also can be used in other ways in service and retail operations. A 'footfall' chart is often used in retail businesses to get a picture of when customers and potential customers are present.

CONTROL CHARTS

Let's now move into the realm of the quality professional. This section on control charts and the next section on process capability are most suited to advanced users of quality tools, who are working with a quality expert. The key point about using a control chart is that you need to have defined what normal levels of time are required to deliver a particular service. What is 'normal', what is 'high' and what is 'low' time required?

Imagine you were working in a bank credit department and trying to service mortgage applications. How long should it take to process an application? How can you classify the different types of applications? By looking at the norms, high and low levels, it then becomes clear whether the process is running well or whether there are other elements that are getting in the way of the smooth running on the process. If the process is seen to be going beyond the Upper or Lower limits, then there is a need to find out what is causing this, either good or bad, and find ways to address any issues.

The control chart is a development of the run chart, in which, using statistical methods, upper and lower control limits are determined. These limits are calculated using data gathered while the process is operating normally. Any adjustments made should be normal ones rather than remedial ones.

An example of a control chart with control and working limits is shown in **Figure 11.16**.

FIGURE 11.16: CONTROL CHART

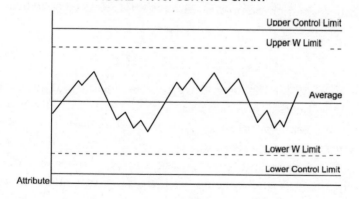

The use of statistical process control (SPC) through control charts can be very useful in a business where a large number of transactions take place – for example, a bank.

Statistical process control removes discussion from the realm of opinion firmly into the arena of facts. By improving the process, it becomes possible to reduce the gap between the upper and lower limits and to be assured that the process is operating to acceptable levels of performance.

A process is said to be in statistical control if a number of criteria are satisfied:

- No value lies outside the control limits;
- No more than about one in 40 values lies between the warning and control limits;
- No examples of two consecutive values lie in the same warning zone;
- No runs of more than six values lie either side of the average line;
- No runs of more than six values are all rising or all falling.

Be careful, however, when using SPC, to understand what the charts are actually saying. If the process is running between the upper and lower limits, this only means that the process is running *consistently*, it does not necessarily mean that the service is being delivered to the required specification.

With the process under control, we can now turn our attention to determining whether the process can meet the required specification.

PROCESS CAPABILITY

The attention so far has been on processes and how they work in their own right. But processes are put in place to deliver on an objective, to meet a specification. A question that needs to be asked is whether the process is able to do what you think it should be able to do. This is an important question because sometimes too much is expected of people and systems – which can lead to failures. If the system is not able to deliver on your promise to your customers, you will end up with dissatisfied customers and simply are creating an opportunity for your competitors to fill.

Where a control chart shows whether a process is under control, a capability chart shows whether the process can consistently meet the specification requirements.

When a business starts to use process capability, it needs the input of quality professionals, as this can be a complex area, and is really beyond the scope of this section (**Chapter 18**).

Case Study 3: First Steps in Continuous Improvement

At Deutsche Post DHL (DPDHL), process improvement has been high on the agenda for many years. DPDHL's division, DHL Supply Chain (DSC) Europe, deploys a group of so-called 'advisors', who are trained as 'black belts' and follow a structured approach to improve and intensively support DSC warehouses all over Europe. Success has delivered increased productivity, costs savings, satisfied customers and involved employees. This, however, is just one side of the coin of improvement: event- or project-driven and depending on experts to facilitate it.

But more than 80% of the problems faced day-to-day can be solved by the teams working in the processes without the help of an expert. The key question is how to involve everybody and to improve every day – to continuously improve the small problems before they get bigger.

This ambition to take the next step towards continuous improvement was recognised by the country board in Turkey and so a pilot was started at one of the distribution centres near Istanbul. Even bigger questions then were raised: how to implement a culture of continuous improvement? And what is a culture of continuous improvement?

In order to improve, you need to know where you are – your current condition – and where you want to go – your future condition. The pilot was based on these two questions.

In a workshop, the site management team discussed DSC's strategic targets and what these meant for their operation. Problems were identified and a clear direction was set. During the kick-off meeting, the site manager explained the direction and the change that was needed to all employees.

The next step was to identify the current condition and to start monitoring the process performance. The current key performance indicators (KPIs) were reviewed and all process owners were asked what they needed to know to be confident that their process and team was doing well.

But KPIs and monitoring are not enough; everybody needs to know the team's performance and whether this is on target. So a Performance Dialogue was developed. On daily / shift basis, each team leader discusses the process performance of the previous day. How was our productivity – on target? What was our quality – any mistakes, complaints? Did we deliver on time? And even more important, how safe is our work environment? Accidents and near accidents were measured and *via* the 'team barometer' the team members could indicate their mood and motivation. All these 5 KPIs were visualised on the Performance Dialogue Board, using simple green (on target) and red (not on target) indicators.

Creating a dialogue in which all employees are involved and contribute is not an easy task. The team leaders were trained in asking the right questions and intensively coached during several weeks.

After this routine of performance dialogue was established, the next step was developing problem-solving skills in the team. Once a problem was identified, the root cause needs to be found and countermeasures defined. All issues and suggestions were registered on the board, including 'who' and 'when', visible to everybody. Whatever the team could not solve by themselves was escalated to the next level Performance Dialogue by the team leader. The following day, he immediately informed his team about the outcome regarding the issue.

In this way, a cycle of continuous improvement was created: monitoring and discussing the performance, identifying the issues and suggestions to improve, root cause analysis and implementing the countermeasures. The support of an advisor was called in to support only in relation to complex problems.

Implementing this new routine was not easy. Many old habits needed to be broken and team members had to gain confidence to bring up problems and suggestions.

After a period of trial and error, the team leaders and their teams found the right way of working and started to further develop the dialogue, the visual management and problem-solving. Tangible results proved that they were on the right track: increased employee satisfaction (over 20%) and increased productivity (over 10%).

Some of the lessons we learned were:

• Continuous improvement requires the involvement of everybody and of all levels – the role modelling attitude of the site manager was key;

• Developing problem-solving capability is the heart of continuous improvement;

- To change old habits into new routines takes time, effort and coaching and must be done with respect;
- Being involved is fun and motivating; motivated people deliver good results.

12: Employee Involvement

People are probably the most important resource of an effective service organisation. It is through the efforts and creativity of people that customer and client needs are serviced and future innovative responses are developed. People are needed to run and develop office processes, distribution processes and sales processes.

If people are so centrally important to the delivery of services to customers, it is clear that they need to be involved in the improvement activities. In a company following the principles of Lean Service, people are required to *think* as well as *do*. The Lean Service approach relies upon the active involvement of people in the improvement process, and the team approach is the common means of delivering on this.

People need to be trained in how teams work, and how they can learn to work together to solve problems. The tools and techniques of team-building are addressed in this chapter, although not all problems require the use of teams – many can be addressed by individuals.

Nonetheless, the real challenge for management today is to harness the full potential of their people, to capture and channel their efforts to achieve the goals and objectives of the business. People need leadership and often want to be part of something good and worthwhile. People working in a business all share a common goal, to serve the customer but also to support their own lifestyles through their efforts. This can best be achieved through the mutual development of the capability of a business to meet and exceed customer needs and wants.

COMPANY CULTURE

The culture of a company or organisation is largely dependent on its leadership. People in a business respond depending on how they perceive the requirements of management. If managers have an open, positive attitude to developing their operations, working with their people to deliver this, then most staff will respond positively. If managers adopt a closed, autocratic style, then staff will respond by taking cover, protecting themselves and generally being unwilling to participate in improvement activities. People want to be involved; they want to contribute; they want to be respected and valued; and they want to feel they are doing a good job. This is true for all levels of people within an organisation.

Managers decide which style of operation they want to manage. Many managers believe they are the only ones capable of doing the job 'right' – the old adage 'if you want a job done right, then you need to do it yourself' seems to be their motto. If this is true, then the business has a serious problem because even the very best individuals are limited by the amount of hours in the day.

Before deciding which type of business management style to adopt, it can be useful to ask what could be achieved if there were others with the same focus and commitment working in the business? Imagine if, rather than having just one capable, enthusiastic and committed person, there were 10 or 20 or 100, all working for the same goal, all doing their best. The real challenge facing management is to give the others in a business a shared goal, an objective that they can work towards and help deliver. This can be difficult to achieve but the rewards are certainly worthwhile. Remember that the manager, the leader, sets the culture.

The importance of management's role in this area cannot be over-stated. If the people in a business are to deliver to their true potential, then management must create and sustain an environment where staff's contributions are both sought and recognised. Management sets the values by which the business operates. If the values are set high, then staff are likely to aspire to meet them. If the value system of the business is set low, then the business is very likely to meet that low target too. It is important to realise while the emphasis here is on managers taking a lead role in developing the values of the organisation and sharing those values with all staff, there is a definite requirement on staff to engage with the values and to align themselves with them.

This concept of a business value system underpinned by respect, respect for its people, its customers and society is very well summed up in a phrase often used by Liam Lacey of Tanco Engineering, used to describe the value system of his business, and shown in **Figure 12.1**.

FIGURE 12.1: A VALUE SYSTEM

	Fairness, Firmness, Consistency.
	Liam Lacey, Tanco Engineering
Fairness	Everyone is entitled to be treated fairly. A balance needs to be struck between the needs of individuals and the business.
Firmness	When policy has been decided upon and defined, it will be followed.
Consistency	The same rules apply to all.

What is the alternative to this approach of Fairness, Firmness and Consistency? Perhaps the old saying 'The beatings will continue until morale improves' could describe the counter-approach. Which approach will be used within an operation is definitely a decision and not a given. The management and staff effectively decide together how they will work together.

APPROPRIATE STRUCTURES

The way businesses are structured can have a major impact on how staff respond and how they work.

The traditional approach to business organisation led to specialisation and departmentalisation at management levels, as in **Figure 12.2**. The accountant took control of the finances, the finance department and the finance staff. The sales manager took control of, and responsibility for, the sales function and the sales and sales support staff. The manufacturing manager, likewise, took control of manufacturing and all that entails. This departmentalised approach leads to the creation of a typical organisation chart.

FIGURE 12.2: AN ORGANISATION CHART

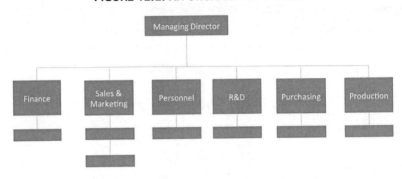

People are placed within the organisation according to their expertise and experience. The financial matters are handled by, and in, the finance department; the same is true of each of the other departments. This approach can be effective and efficient, if all the work to be done by a department is under the control of the department. However, this is often not the case.

How many customers' needs are addressed by any one department in a business? Let's take a simple example to illustrate this point, where a customer wants to place an order for a standard product, as in **Figure 12.3**.

FIGURE 12.3: PLACING AN ORDER

1. The sales person visits the customer and receives the order. The completed order docket is brought back to the office and handed to the order entry clerk.
2. The order entry clerk enters the order in the "system" and delivers the daily sales report to the sales manager.
3. The next day the daily sales sheets are transferred to Warehousing.
4. Warehousing has four of the five items ordered in stock, so they place an order to the wholesaler for the out-of-stock item.
5. Warehousing then prepare the other four items for shipping and send the paperwork to Finance for invoicing.
6. The wholesaler telephones warehousing to say that the order will be delayed for three weeks.

Meanwhile, Finance informs Warehousing that the customer is on hold due to an outstanding bill and advises them not to ship the four items they have already picked. Warehousing tells Sales, and so it goes on.

Each of these inter-departmental communications takes time and leads to delays in meeting customer needs.

The same process map can be carried out for each of the many customer-related and supplier-related interactions within a business. The resulting physical flow and process flow maps will help to identify wastes.

Arranging the structure of the business differently, along process rather than departmental lines, might remove significant delays and wastes. A revised structure is presented in **Figure 12.4**.

Here, staff are allocated to areas of the business according to business need. Some finance staff are located in the sales and purchasing areas, and thus they can identify quickly which customers may cause problems and can make sure that key suppliers are paid on time, ensuring availability of materials. The departmental heads are still in place, ensuring a professional approach is maintained and that the management team retains a coherent approach to managing the business. This process-oriented structure removes many wastes from the operation and helps to build understanding and team work within the business.

FIGURE 12.4: THE ORGANISATION STRUCTURE - DEVELOPED

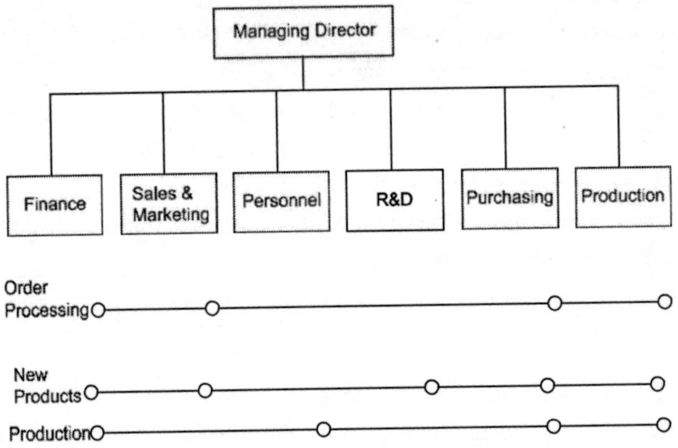

TEAM-BUILDING

An earlier chapter looked at the four stages of team-building:

- Forming;
- Storming;
- Norming;
- Performing.

Now let's look at the more practical aspects of how teams are built. There are a number of basic steps to be followed when forming teams, the most obvious of which is deciding whether a team is required to achieve the result. Not all tasks need a team to address them. Some tasks are better handled by individuals, focused to achieve results. However, once it has been decided that the scale of the task needs a team to solve it, the process of team-building can begin.

Team Selection

Teams are formed to solve problems or develop processes, because of the benefits of having more than one brain working on the problem.

It is important that the chosen team members bring something of value to the team. Their knowledge, skills and experience should be relevant to the task facing the team. There is usually very little point in having the accounts person join a team focused on developing the sales process. By the same token, if the team is focused on addressing problems with customer complaints, then the team should have representatives from sales, production, quality and finance, to ensure that the full response of the company is brought to bear on such a wide-ranging issue.

Team Leadership

Effective team leadership is critical. The leader needs to find ways to build on the strengths and abilities of the team members in an effort to achieve the goals and objectives of the team, and the business. The team leader needs to know about and understand the basic LB tools and techniques and to be able to transfer this understanding to the team members. The leader needs to be familiar with brainstorming, be capable of negotiating, and be able to deal with inter-personal issues. The leader needs to be driven to achieve the goals of the team and also able to lead and drive the team as circumstances demand.

Positive interaction between team members is critical to the success of a team. The leader needs to create an environment where creativity of team members can flourish and where ideas and innovations are developed and worked to the point that they contribute to achieving the overall team objectives. The leader needs to ensure that all team members contribute to the task at hand. The leader needs to be sensitive to the personalities in the team, to ensure the vibrant personalities do not drown out the quieter ones. The team needs to learn the art of active listening, realising that some people do not like to take a leading role but that they very often have something positive to contribute.

The leader needs to ensure that the team bases its decisions on facts rather than opinions. The basic quality tools of check sheets and run charts can be helpful in this regard. And finally, the leader needs to help the team develop to the point where it takes responsibility for its own actions. The team needs to be strong enough to accept challenges and to deliver on them.

Team Objectives

A team needs an objective, a reason for existence. Without an objective how can the team members know they have completed their job? How can managers be sure the team is doing valuable work rather than just wasting time? The objective set for a team helps to give the team focus and helps the team leader to direct energies to particular tasks. As the team is likely to be in place for an extended period of time, the objective helps ensure that progress is made towards an overall goal. Without an objective, people can wander from the subject and lose sight of why the team was formed in the first place.

The objectives being set for the team need to be:

- **Realistic:** There is little point in asking a newly-formed team to solve problems that are unrealistic. The scale and scope of the problem to be tackled needs to be matched with the resources devoted to it;

- **Achievable:** The team should have a reasonable chance of success. If management sets the goals too high, then the team is unlikely to achieve them. A failure at the early stages of team-building has negative long-term implications. It is generally better to set a slightly lower goal and to achieve it than to set a very high goal and fail;

- **Demanding:** While the goals being set for the team should not be set too high, they need to be set high enough to ensure that staff will have to work to achieve them. If the goal is too low, then people are unlikely to engage with the process.

Team Meetings

The team needs to meet, to discuss progress, develop action plans, to talk through problems encountered and successes achieved. The meetings should be kept relatively short and structured. The use of a simple agenda, recording action points, progress and future activities can be helpful.

Meetings can serve three very useful purposes:

- Report on action to date;

- Discuss potential solutions to outstanding problems;
- Plan future action.

The leader should focus the meetings on identifying solutions, as a team, to outstanding issues. Meetings also can be used to develop a team understanding of key tools and techniques as they become relevant.

Meetings should be kept relatively informal at the early stages of the process, in an effort to build a group approach to problem-solving. As the team develops, and people learn how to work together, the process can move to being more formal, with minutes and detailed agenda items. Minutes should be short, to the point and focused on directing future activity, and should be issued very soon after the meeting, not later than next day if at all possible.

Team Assignments

Teams are created to *do* things, to deliver on specific objectives and to achieve goals. A team of people that meet, discuss problems and do not deliver on them is just another waste in a business. Once the objectives of the team have been set, it should become possible to identify specific tasks and actions that need to be completed before the objectives can be achieved.

Specific tasks need to be assigned to individual team members or pairs of members. These people then have the responsibility to deliver on these tasks to, and for, the team. By harnessing the energies of several people to different facets of the problem, the team can deliver results more quickly than any one individual could.

The order in which tasks are tackled, and the priorities given to the tasks, needs to be discussed and agreed at the team meetings. This approach ensures that a coherent response is developed, and that everybody knows how their individual efforts will contribute to achieving the overall objectives of the team.

Team Results and Reviews

The results and progress being made by the team need to be reviewed regularly. This review should take place at two levels:

- Within the team itself;
- By senior management.

The team needs to be aware of the results it is achieving. The team should not have to wait for management, or the finance department, or any other outside element of the organisation, to tell them whether they are performing well or achieving positive results. This self-review should be incorporated into the regular team meetings and become a natural part of the team's activities. As the team reaches the objectives and goals set for it, it has the opportunity of suggesting even higher objectives based on their shared learning and the benefit of the experience they have gained as a team.

The second level of results review should take place between the team and senior management. If management felt it important enough to commit company staff and resources to tackle a problem by forming a team, then management should be interested in the progress of the team. Management should seek to review progress, to be informed of actions taken and results achieved. Management should be interested enough in the activities of the team to ask about future activities and when and how the team sees itself achieving its objectives. Management need to care about the progress of the team and need to let the team members know that they care. Some managers fall into the trap of derogating responsibility for the team and its objectives completely to the team leader. While this is legitimate up to a point, managers still need to demonstrate that the efforts of the team are aligned with the overall objectives of the business and that the team's efforts are both worthwhile and valued.

The team, along with management, should identify a number of key measures that can be used to monitor progress. These measures need to be chosen carefully to ensure that they are a true indicator of progress and also that, by achieving improvement in them, no other adverse affects are felt by the business.

There are a number of general points to be made about data and measures:

- **Record data:** The systematic capture of data from processes can help focus attention of staff on the facts of a business. By recording say, 'sales per day', people can be directed towards identifying ways of achieving improvement. The old adage of 'what get measured improves' is still true;

- **Analyse data:** Look for information from the raw data. Are there patterns? What do the numbers show? By choosing carefully what data is recorded, new ways to improve the operation can be found. The needs and desires of customers can often provide a guide to what should be measured. Are clients focused on timeliness of delivery, superior quality or purely on price?

- **Use data:** If people have gone to the bother of identifying good measures for the team's work, it is vitally important to act based on the results and data captured. The data is useful to the business only when used to further improve the operations.

BRAINSTORMING

Brainstorming is one of the most widely-known tools used by teams. The earlier focus was on silent brainstorming; let's look now at the more traditional form. The approach is based on the positive interaction between team members when focused on tackling particular problems or issues. The team is brought together usually in a relatively confined space and is given a limited amount of time.

A number of conditions need to be set before a team can embark on a successful brainstorming session:

- **All team members are equal:** Normal levels of status within the organisation should be suspended during the session. Each member of the team has a potentially equal contribution to make;

- **All ideas are equal:** The process, at least in the first phase, is non-judgemental. Ideas are sought without determining whether they are practical or even feasible. Experience has shown that an idea that was, of itself, impractical can often lead to the creation of another feasible idea that might not otherwise have arisen;

- **All comments must be positive:** The process is designed to help the team identify and capture ideas. There is an onus on all team members to be positive towards each other and their suggestions. The time for critical analysis is during phase two of the process.

Armed with these general conditions, the team can move to initiate the brainstorming activity. It is generally necessary to remove the team from distractions during the process. This is often best achieved by taking the team 'off-site', away from the daily demands of business. At a minimum, the session should take place in a room without telephones and without a window overlooking the business.

The full brainstorming process consists of three distinct phases:

- Idea generation;
- Critical analysis;
- Implementation planning.

Phase I – Idea Generation

The idea generation phase is the core of creativity in the brainstorming process. The objective is to focus the creative energy of the team on finding ideas that may contribute to solving the problems facing the team. The problem(s) to be addressed are written on flipchart sheets, usually attached to the walls of the room so that they are in view of the team members. Even though they may not be concentrating on the sheets, the sheets often act as triggers for further ideas.

The brainstorming session should be time limited, typically to 20 to 30 minutes per creative session. The leader of the session usually offers a number of ideas to start the process and they work with the other team members to draw out ideas and suggestions from all the team members. The task of writing suggestions on the flipcharts should be shared between a number of people, to both facilitate participation and also to give the writer a break.

Where necessary, refreshments should be brought to the brainstorming room rather than breaking for food. This forced proximity with the team and the problem helps engender a highly focused environment, conducive to the generation of ideas.

When the flow of ideas has dried up, and the leader feels that a reasonable number of ideas or suggestions have been gathered, the first phase can be drawn to a conclusion.

Phase II – Critical Analysis

The brainstorming team has now created a number of sheets containing ideas and suggestions. Some of these may be very practical, some may not. Phase II focuses on rating the ideas.

A simple rating system looks at the ideas under four headings:

- **Definite:** Ideas that can, and should, be implemented immediately. These ideas are immediately beneficial and often arise simply by giving people the opportunity to make suggestions or through the interaction between people from different areas of the business;

- **Probable:** Ideas that probably would work and be of benefit, but which require some further study or development before they could be implemented;

- **Possible:** These ideas may or may not work. They may have some chance of success but it is unlikely;

- **Unlikely:** Generally, off-the-wall ideas that have arisen during the session. While being unlikely in themselves, they may have contributed to the thought process of the team and helped to release other more likely suggestions.

When the team has rated the ideas, it moves on to Phase III.

Phase III – Implementation Planning

An idea that is not acted upon is a lost opportunity.

The team has rated the ideas and generally will focus on those rated as 'Definite' or 'Probable'. The challenge now facing the team is to prioritise the ideas, and to identify the necessary time and resources required to move from the ideas stage to implementation.

The team will develop an implementation plan to identify resources and responsibilities. The plan grows to become the action plan for the team and can provide both the team and management with a clear and measurable plan for action.

Getting Close to the Action

While brainstorming usually takes place in a closed environment, away from the distractions of the 'day job', another approach also can work: bring the team to the problem. Bringing the team to the office area, the sales area, the manufacturing area or wherever the problem exists often can help people to understand the issues more clearly. Some people, particularly general office staff or shop floor workers, find it more effective and efficient to demonstrate the practical issues they face in the delivery of their job than to try and vocalise the issues.

Practical experience has shown that bringing the team to the problem can be very effective. People can see clearly that the daily problems they are experiencing and dealing with are receiving attention and they often contribute further ideas to solve the problem.

Case Study 4: Parker Advertising

Parker Advertising is a small family-owned business that provides advertising and marketing support to businesses. The advertising world is fast-paced, with very short deadlines and customers who expect creativity on demand. The business model is based on being able to deliver creativity, on demand and at pace, consistently. Parker Advertising employs seven staff and is structured as a number of departments: Customer Service / Account Management; Artwork; Script writing / Copy; and Administration/Accounts.

The big issue facing the company was 'How can a small team deliver creative material to a number of demanding clients, at short lead times, consistently, while facing competition from much bigger organisations?'.

The company moved forward through discussion with the key department leads. It was clear that a lot of energy was devoted to firefighting and rapidly-changing priorities.

The company moved to develop a jobs board, where each job was represented on a horizontal line and each department as a vertical column.

Each morning, the department heads would meet to discuss and agree the priorities for the day and update each other on current status, issues, ideas and priorities.

The use of this visual planning board addressed the need for accurate information on job status, priorities and issues. Its use helped the team to focus on producing output and took away the tedium of constantly looking for updates. By agreeing on priorities collectively, there was a reduction in job priority changes, leading to increased creative output and better serviced clients.

13: Lean Sales

How do you sell? Do you have a technique? Are you a 'happy chappie' who talks about the match and takes an order or are you the serious type who focuses only on the technical aspects of your service or product and the customer's needs? If there is more than one person selling for an organisation, is there a common understanding of what the business sells and how to sell it?

It is often thought that selling is a black art. Yes, there are some really exceptional sales people but there are also many ordinary people who can benefit from the application of some 'science' to the 'art' of selling.

Put simply, a Company sells its services or products to a Customer, against Competitors and in a specific environment, or Community, as shown in **Figure 13.1**.

FIGURE 13.1: SALES STRATEGY

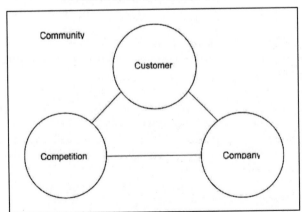

Now let's look at each of these four 'Cs' to understand better how Lean principles can be applied to the sales process.

YOUR COMPANY

One of the most basic elements of any good sales process is that the sales person needs to know and to understand the service offering and the capabilities of the business. Unless the sales person knows these details, they are likely to over-sell or under-sell the business and the offering. This knowledge requirement can be addressed through the use of a company profile sheet, as in **Figure 13.2**.

FIGURE 13.2: COMPANY PROFILE

Location			
No. Employees			
Turnover			
Profit			
GOOD POINTS			
Key Services	**Service Delivery Process**	**Sales / Marketing**	**Finance**
1			
2			
3			
WEAK POINTS			
Key Services	**Service Delivery Process**	**Sales / Marketing**	**Finance**
1			
2			
3			
Key Actions	**Service Delivery Process**	**Sales / Marketing**	**Finance**
1			
2			
3			

The company profile sheet captures key facts about the business. By looking at the key services and seeking strengths and weaknesses in them, an objective picture of the offering is formed. The focus on particular aspects of the service – such as the service itself, a uniqueness in meeting customer needs, special market position or financial advantage such as cost – helps the individuals in the business to look again at what they already 'know' about the service.

If a number of people complete the profile sheet independently of each other and then review the sheets together, different opinions are likely to be expressed regarding strengths and weaknesses. These differences of opinion can provide a very rich opportunity for discussion and often can lead to the identification of key actions.

The profile sheet ends with a list of key actions. The whole Lean approach is focused on improvement – this is equally relevant in the sales process. The identification of key actions can be the accentuation of positive points or the minimisation of weaknesses. Quite often, the actions are a combination of both.

The detail of the headings under strengths and weaknesses will depend on what type of business is being run. The decision as to what headings should be included in the profile sheet can form the basis for a worthwhile discussion, helping people to focus objectively on the business as an entity – one that can be improved. Additional information can be appended to the profile sheet as more detail on the business is gathered – outlining, for example, process capabilities, assets, and competitive advantages.

Before moving on to look at customer, competitor and community profiles, let's look at both service lists and customer lists, to capture an overview of the current situation for the business.

SERVICES LIST

Few businesses have a single service. In general, sales are made up by a range of services or at least from a set of variations on the basic offering. The services list captures information on these offerings with a view to identifying which services are of most significance to the business, as in **Figure 13.3**.

FIGURES 13.3: SERVICES LIST

Services	Sales Value Last Year €	Profit Last Year €	Difficulty	Rating
1.				
2.				
3.				
4.				
5.				
6.				

The services list should include all major services offered by the company as well as identifying variations. In some businesses, the services list can run to several pages. All the variety of offerings should be listed to show the levels of complexity inherent in such cases.

The services list seeks to capture sales value, as well as profitability per offering or at least contribution levels. The 'Difficulty' column seeks to determine just how difficult it is for the business to offer that particular service or to scale delivery. The 'Rating' column is once again relatively subjective. The aim is to balance profitability, volume and difficulty to identify priorities for focus for the business.

CUSTOMER LIST

The customer list format is very similar to the services list. The list seeks to identify a rating for customers to allow a degree of classification to be applied, as in **Figure 13.4**.

Sales volume and profitability measures can help in this classification process. By applying the Pareto (80 / 20) principle, customers can be classified as A, B, or C type. The objective once again is to help a business to prioritise its limited resources, to identify classes of customers or areas of business that are both high volume and high profitability, and to help identify areas for future potential growth based on the shared experience of the members of the business.

FIGURE 13.4: CUSTOMER LIST

Customers	Sales Value Last Year €	Profit Last Year €	Difficulty of Doing Business	Rating
1.				
2.				
3.				
4.				
5.				
6.				

A customer list can usually be generated from the accounts system by listing customers in terms of annual sales invoiced. This data can then be added to, in order to address the other areas listed on the customer list.

Customer Profile

It really is important to know who the customers are. Many people sell to the *wants* of their customers but seldom address their *needs*. If only customers' wants are addressed, then there is a risk of missing their needs and leaving the door open to the competition.

Customer needs can be determined only through discussion with, and analysis of, customers. It is important to try and capture the 'voice of the customer', first-hand, to better understand their needs and wants. Ethnographic tools can be used to get close to the customer, to see and experience how the services are used to give yourself an opportunity to 'see' potential needs that can be addressed.

It is important to try and capture the voice of the customer first-hand, rather than based on studies carried out by third parties. Companies such as Harley-Davidson support rallies and gatherings of their customers across the USA and worldwide to do just this. Their offering has evolved from pure motorcycle manufacture to more of a life-style offering. To deliver this new offering effectively, H-D had to understand the lifestyles of their clients, in their many different ways. In the long-term, selling to meet customer needs is the only sustainable approach.

A customer profile sheet is a useful tool in helping determine the needs of clients. Many sales people feel they 'know' their clients and have no need to commit this knowledge to paper. If the business is to grow and develop, a shared understanding of the customer base needs to be developed, which is not possible if the information is kept in sales people's heads or personal files. The customer profile sheet helps with this process, as in **Figure 13.5**.

FIGURE 13.5: CUSTOMER PROFILE

Customer Name			
Rating			
Location			
No Employees			
Telephone			
Fax			
Email			
Web			
Turnover (estimated)			
Profit (estimated)			
KEY SERVICES	Last Year	This Year	Potential
1			
2			
3			
4			
5			
6			

The sheet seeks to capture some basic information on key customers, such as where they are located, how many people they employ as well, as estimates of annual turnover and profitability. Information on what products or services they bought last year is also useful, along with an estimate of their expected purchasing in the year ahead. The objective is to arrive at a 'Rating' for the customer. This rating is an indication of how important, or otherwise, the customer is to the business. The overall objective is clearly to provide the business with an objective, consensus view on a priority list of customers, who are serviced very well given their importance to the company.

Customer profile sheets should be completed at least for the business' top customers, the top 20% of customers who account for 80% of sales, the 'A' customers. These can easily be identified by referring to the customer list.

If there are other customers who could grow to significance, then it is obviously worthwhile to include them in the process and prepare customer profiles for them also.

COMPETITOR PROFILE

A competitor profile is largely based on the same format as the company profile. The sheet captures the same data but this time for key competitors. The objectivity of the process often helps to identify weaknesses in a competitor's service offering that were not previously obvious.

In some cases, the sharing of information on competitors in this structured way can lead to the piecing together of different elements of a jigsaw. When everybody's little piece of the puzzle is brought together, a clear picture of the true level of competition can be gained.

The objectives of the process are:

- To understand the competition in comparison to the company itself;
- To pool the knowledge held within different elements of the business;
- To plan responses to tackle the competition in an effective and efficient way.

The competition is just that, competition for business. They are trying to take sales away from our business – the winner is the one who takes most!

COMMUNITY PROFILE

The community profile, or environmental analysis, is possibly the hardest profile sheet to complete. It's hard to foretell the future but this is what you are trying to do here. By limiting the view forward to three to five years, you have a better chance of getting our predictions right. For example, changes in European Union laws do not arrive overnight – there is usually a significant period of discussion and consultation as changes are proposed. It is important to be aware of changes as they are being proposed if they could affect, either positively or negatively, your future business potential.

The increasing emphasis on environmental control and pollution minimisation is a case in point. For many businesses, these changes in the law simply add to the burden of doing business while, for a small number of other businesses, they provide a source of new sales opportunities.

By looking at social and economic factors, it may be possible to identify in advance potential changes in market demand. The demographics in Ireland indicate that the 50+ year-old market will become very significant over the coming years with related business potential. Such changes in demographics and buying power can lead to real market opportunities. The challenge is to identify these opportunities and prepare an offering to benefit from them.

PROFILE ANALYSIS

The work of preparing profiles on the company, customers, competitors and community has been done. The time for analysis is now. The use of visual techniques can help here.

Attach your company profile to a wall; on one side of it, attach your key customer profiles; on the other side, attach your key competitor profiles; and below, attach your community profile. Now study the information you have gathered.

The primary objective of the exercise is to increase sales and profitability. A commonly-accepted fact of sales is that it is very much harder to get a new customer than it is to sell to an existing one. An analysis of the customer profiles may lead to the realisation that some existing customers are not buying all of the range of services that they could. The opportunity may arise either to increase the range of services being sold to individual customers or to offer higher margin services.

Turning attention to your competitor profiles, it should be possible to identify action items, where advantage can be taken in the market. By examining the key customers serviced by the competition, it may be possible to identify prospects, customers who already have a need for a service similar to those that your business can supply but who are buying from competitors. Care needs to be exercised as to how competitors are tackled; if they are stronger, then avoid 'enraging the bull' rather than securing new business.

The last part of the puzzle relates to your community profile. By looking at this profile, it may be possible to identify strategic decisions and directions that the company needs to take.

COMPETITIVE ANALYSIS

Your company and competitor analysis sheets can be used to start the process of competitive analysis. To take customers from competitors, it is essential that competitive advantage is identified in your service offerings. The competitive analysis sheet helps with this process (see **Figure 13.6**).

The competitive analysis process is widely used by major corporations. A joke in the automotive industry is that the first 10 cars from any production run are bought not by customers but by competitors. These cars are then tested and dis-assembled to see what new ideas have been developed. The objective is not simply to copy but to learn from others – by examining carefully the solutions of others to innovate further and to build increased functionality or performance into products.

A good starting point for competitive analysis is the advertising materials, brochures and specification sheets produced by competitors. Careful study of these often can challenge a team to deliver at least as good performance as the competition.

FIGURE 13.6: COMPETITIVE ANALYSIS

	Estimated Sales	Estimated Market Position	Key Features
Competitor 1			
Competitor 2			
Competitor 3			
Your Company			
Areas of Competitive Advantage			
A.			
B.			
C.			
Areas of Competitive Disadvantage			
A.			
B.			
Actions Identified			**Priority**
1.			
2.			
3.			

The competitive analysis process should not be limited to sales and marketing staff but should be a team-based activity involving sales, design, purchasing, operations and finance staff. This team approach will help to ensure that a company-wide response to the challenge of competitors is realised. Take the opportunity to scrutinise competitor services at trade fairs and exhibitions and to identify both strengths and weaknesses of their services or their companies. The challenge is to attack weaknesses and find defences against their strengths.

The 'market worth' tool can be useful when trying to understand market conditions and the relative positions of competitors and competing services. An example of how this tool is used is presented in both tabular and graphical forms in **Figure 13.7**.

FIGURE 13.7: MARKET WORTH

Feature	Competitor's service	Your service	Sales
Price	20,000	23,000	
Power	150HP	165HP	
Capacity	10T	10.5T	
Annual Sales	250	100	

This analysis indicates that the market prefers cheap price to higher specifications, or at least is not prepared to pay much of a premium for those additional features.

SALES MANUAL

The sales process can be developed and improved. The creation of a sales manual often can help salespeople to reach an acceptable level of performance within a reasonable time. Much of the material already gathered is used as a basis for the manual.

At a minimum, the manual should contain:

- Company profile;
- Customer needs, issues and possible solutions;
- Competitor profiles, identifying strengths and weaknesses;
- Technical data and comparison sheets;
- Specification sheets, identifying key order parameters to ensure that the service ordered and delivered is correct;
- Options lists;
- Pricing information and conditions of trade.

SALES FORECASTING

Very few salespeople like to produce sales forecasts. If a sales forecast is asked for, the likely response is that it is impossible to predict the future, so it is impossible to create an accurate sales forecast. However, how can purchasing or operations staff have services ready for sale unless they have some forward visibility of market requirements? If it is not possible for the sales people to produce a forecast, given their closeness to the market, then it is even less possible for someone working in purchasing to do so. The logical conclusion to this argument is to quote extra-long lead-times to customers or to hold large stocks of materials. Imagine going into a restaurant and ordering a chicken dinner only to be told that you had to wait until the egg hatched? Neither solution is favoured by the majority of businesses. It is a necessary fact of life that sales forecasts are made.

In an effort to start the forecasting process, past sales history can be helpful. The services list you created earlier can provide this. Consider whether history is likely to repeat itself, or have factors changed that will significantly change likely sales into the future. Has a new competitor joined the market or have innovative new services been introduced? Will sales promotions be repeated or will new ones be introduced? These factors should be used to modify, if necessary, the sales history information.

The question of what sales are forecast for the coming year also can be asked from this starting point. The creation of an annual sales forecast is useful for purchasing, operations and logistics personnel. It helps them plan for the future with suppliers and infrastructure as well as preparing staff and equipment. However, the annual sales forecast is of little benefit as a regular management tool. Sales management needs to be more immediate and in better control than that allowed by an annual sales forecast.

The forecasting and management of the sales process should happen on a regular basis – daily, weekly or monthly, depending on the type of business. Some businesses, in particular the fast moving consumer goods industry, even measure sales per hour rates. In a more typical environment, weekly monitoring of sales made and prospects forward is usually sufficient. Prospects should be rated, say as ABC, with A prospects being likely to convert to sales and C prospects less likely as short-term sales. Reviews should take place quickly and regularly of progress towards targets and movement on the prospects list. Bar charts can be used quite effectively to monitor progress towards overall targets with weekly sales or individual sales being recorded, depending on the culture of the business (see **Figure 13.8**).

FIGURE 13.8: SALES TARGETS

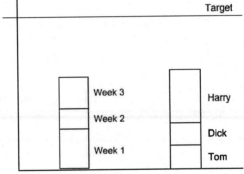

It is essential to review forecast *versus* actual accuracy levels regularly. There is no point in individual sales people forecasting huge sales levels and not delivering on them. By the same token, the opposite situation is almost as bad, where sales are forecast at too low a level. In either situation, procurement, operations and logistics staff will encounter severe problems of too much or too little stock or time or resources to service the customer. Here again, the use of a run chart can be very helpful to record the level of accuracy of forecast *versus* actual sales. Since it is unrealistic in many businesses to expect forecast accuracies of better than within five to 10 per cent, it is useful to set target lines for accuracy on the chart, as in **Figure 13.9**, to get a fact-based understanding of the forecast accuracy being achieved by the sales team.

FIGURE 13.9: FORECAST ACCURACY

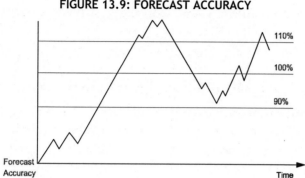

Charting customers' sales patterns was discussed earlier. It often can be very helpful to customers, as well as the business, if customers can be provided with a pattern of their consumption as well as suggested ways to reduce costs along the supply chain between the supplier and the customer.

ACTIVITY PLANNING

When planning a sales strategy, including sales activities, it is important to create an overall plan using a diary. Are there specific events taking place, key industry sector shows or other such activities that require a presence? It is important to spread activities over the year rather than having them all grouped into one particular part of the year, unless, of course, the business is purely time-dependent.

The primary goal of such activities is to bring the company and its offering into the minds of customers and prospective customers, and to keep it there. For example, one of the world's largest advertisers is Coca Cola, which constantly reinforces the brand with existing and new customers.

The sales activities should be balanced, including, say, golf or match outings, trade shows and exhibitions, articles in trade journals, advertising and even sponsorship. It is important to capture feedback from customers as to the effectiveness of the activity invested in. There is little point in inviting a customer to a soccer match if they hate the sport. By capturing customer feedback, an activity plan can be developed for future years, working to achieve a positive return from the investment of time and effort.

TARGETING CUSTOMERS

It is usually easier to gain more business from existing customers than it is to capture new ones. Therefore, it is often worth examining what level and type of business is being done with existing customers and to work to maximise this business first. It is helpful to understand the abilities of the business and target sectors or customers where the business has a proven expertise.

When new customers need to be targeted, it is often worthwhile to return to your competitor profile sheets. Are there customers that a particular competitor is doing business with that could be targeted? Set a goal of identifying and securing a specific number of new customers per operating period.

When new prospects have been identified, it is useful to prepare a customer profile sheet for them. Identify, as best as possible, what is important to each customer, what they are looking for that the competition is not providing. Then the business must be challenged to see whether it can service this need. There is no point in making service promises that the company will not be able to meet. There is no point, and indeed a lot of negativity, in raising customer expectations unless they can be met. Imagine if an accountancy firm offered to complete an audit within a given time at a given price but did not have the staff, systems and availability to do so.

Having identified prospects, their needs and the ability to service them, it is time to develop a plan of attack. It is important to be prepared for the response of prospective customers who may look for samples. By preparing for these eventualities, the business will be able to project a professional and efficient image of the business.

MEASURES FOR THE SALES TEAM

Using measures can be helpful when it comes to managing a sales team. Is the salesperson who spends all their time in the car being effective? Is there an opportunity to learn from the best members of the sales team, by sharing and developing a company-wide sales process?

Some of the more obvious measures are those that relate to personal sales made, which are easily tracked, using a run chart to check patterns over time and also in bar chart form to see progress towards a target level. The overall sales level can also be tracked in this way.

An additional twist to sales measurement looks at the variation between list price and actual sales price invoiced. If there is a significant differential, maybe the list price is too high or maybe margin is being given away too easily. Either way, at least by measuring the differential, attention will be drawn to the issue.

Back to your sales person in his / her car. A simple but very interesting measure for someone managing a sales team is the measure of sales made per kilometre driven. This is an effectiveness measure and often can be useful in helping sales staff to realise the opportunities for a more focused approach to selling.

Finally, forecast accuracy is a very important measure from the point of view of the overall business. Sales forecasts should be driven towards being more accurate and also driven to meet the growth needs of the business, putting pressure on sales, design, operations, procurement and logistics staff to meet them.

CUSTOMER SERVICE

Customers have now been landed, so it is essential that the business meets their expectations by providing them with a quality service.

Each customer is different. It is important to recognise these differences and to ensure that systems are developed enough to meet each customer's needs. Key measures should be identified, used and tracked to record performance and developments made in the area of customer service.

For example, as part of your improvement activities, you could track and publicise measures such as:

- On-time deliveries;

- Customer complaints;
- Completed *vs.* partial orders;
- Paperwork complaints.

As improvements are made in each key area, communicate these to customers and to enter into a dialogue to determine how the process can be improved further. This dialogue with customers builds relationships that raise the entry barriers to other competitors. The challenge is to improve the level of operational capability to the point where the business is truly world class, offering services to its customers Quicker, Better and Cheaper. If that is the case, then the customers will stay with the business.

Case Study 5: Customer Service Kaizen at Directski.com

Directski.com, and its subsidiary Ski Beat, organise and sell 'package' ski holidays that include flights from the UK or Ireland, bus transfers from arrival airports to ski resorts, accommodation and in-resort ancillary services. The company found that, while customer service scores were excellent for their overall holiday experience (over 95% would recommend to a friend), it scored relatively poorly on the bus transfer part of the holiday. Arranging the bus transfers also required a high level of administrative effort and, at almost €600k *per annum* in one destination country alone, was one of Directski.com's biggest variable costs.

In early 2011, Directski.com identified bus transfers as a candidate for the company's first major Kaizen event believing that it could:

- Improve customer experience;
- Spend less time planning and managing;
- Lower third-party costs.

The Kaizen event itself took place over two days in September 2011 but was preceded by a significant amount of pre-work and data gathering, including shadowing the bus planning process and joining actual bus transfers.

The Kaizen event was held in the Directski.com's Dublin head office but included employees from the company's operations in UK and France, representing a wide range of departments within the business including sales, operations, technology and finance. The agenda for the two days included:

- Context-setting and review of objectives;
- Refresh on the spirit of improvement, Lean basic principles and applicable tools;

- Current state analysis (three sub-teams, one for each result area);
- Future state implementation planning;
- Develop and plan countermeasures (just-do-its and follow-up plan);
- Standardised work drafting;
- Draft final report, A3 and supporting documentation write-up;
- Celebrate success and recognition.

The Kaizen event was followed by weekly and monthly check-ins and the countermeasures have been reviewed and improved each year since. The countermeasures implemented and results achieved under each result area following the Kaizen event included:

Improved customer experience

- Customer experience map was drafted and service level agreements established with bus companies;
- Number of guests scoring bus transfers 'poor' reduced by 36%.

Less time planning and managing

- Removed waste from the planning process, changed selling rules to avoid re-work and small technology improvements to automatically populate some planning documents;
- 45% reduction in planning time.

Lower third-party costs

- Moved some planning responsibility in-house, re-negotiated flight landing slots to match bus availability, better bus fill rates, fewer mini-buses;
- 32% decrease in costs – worth over €200k per year to the business.

14: Financial Management

Money is important, and the effective and efficient management of money is essential in a competitive business. It is essential that companies using Lean Business techniques use and develop their understanding of financial matters to ensure the development of their businesses. Too often, financial accounts are left unused. Too often, the insights that even a simple analysis of these figures could give are left unseen. This section cannot cover the full extent of financial analysis or financial management but it aims to de-mystify some of the terms used and show how additional value can be gained from professionally-prepared accounts.

As with many aspects of LB, the objective when using financial analysis is to gain a better understanding of the business, how it is progressing and to try to see danger signs at the earliest possible time. If developing dangers can be seen, then counter-measures can be taken, the earlier the better.

This section looks at some of the financial ratios often used by financial analysts, bankers and investors. The effects of a LB initiative on the measures a company can use to monitor performance are addressed also.

RATIO ANALYSIS

If the business has ever applied for a loan or sought to interest an investor in taking an equity stake, then it has most likely been subjected to ratio analysis. Since the end of the 1800s, when large amounts of capital were required to develop America, ratio analysis has been used to determine whether a particular investment proposal was worthwhile. A series of ratios have grown out of this activity.

One key point to remember is that no single measure is enough to determine the performance of a business. A good analyst will identify a number of relevant measures for a given sector or business type, and also will be very interested in trends over time. In order to get meaningful results, at least three years' accounting information is required – two sets of audited accounts provides this.

Key Operational Ratios

The three key operational ratios are:

- **Turnover per Employee** = Sales Revenue / no. employees;
- **Profit per Employee** = (Profit before Interest and Tax) / no. employees;
- **Value added per Employee** = (Sales Revenue – Cost of materials) / no. employees.

These three ratios seek to understand how efficient the business is with its people, and how effective. The first of these measures is often the easiest one to calculate. It gives an indication of the level of effectiveness of staff, and the systems they operate. The absolute figure is not really that important as the norms vary from sector to sector. Management should be focussed on achieving improvements in this ratio, over time. Leading companies, worldwide, achieve improvements in this ratio of 15% to 20% *per annum.*

The second ratio, that of profit per employee, is a challenging measure, especially for companies looking to employ additional staff, particularly in management, support or indirect functions. The challenge is to ensure that the addition of extra payroll costs leads to an improvement in overall profitability.

The third ratio, value added per employee, is a hard measure, especially for sales-oriented businesses or those with a mixture of sales and manufacturing. Stripping out the cost of materials helps focus business attention on what is important for long-term sustainability. If the value-add is low, the challenge is to increase it. This often can lead to the identification of a need to develop new or innovative products or services. If the value-add is high, then the challenge often can be how to protect the business from competitors who may want to take such valuable business away.

Stock Turnover

Stock turnover is easy to calculate and is a good measure of the efficiency of a business in processing materials. The higher the level of stock turns, the more efficient the business is in turning materials into value-added finished goods. The best companies in the world turn stock 50 to 100 times per year.

The ratios here are:

- Opening Stock = A;
- Closing Stock = B;
- Subtotal = A + B;
- Average Stock = (A+B) / 2;
- **Stock turnover** = Cost of Sales / Average Stock.

A focus on stock turns can help in the development of stores / materials / logistics staff. Also, it can help identify the need to develop suppliers. If suppliers can deliver based on real needs ('just-in-time'), then there will be little need to keep large stocks.

The measure also can help to challenge assumptions in terms of sales and to focus the development of worthwhile and accurate forecasts. It should be obvious that, if forecasts are wildly inaccurate, then it will be very difficult for stores staff or suppliers to meet market sales demands without keeping large stocks. Remember, time is money and the longer stock is held, the lower the stock turns number will be and the more costly it will be to run and develop the business.

Debtor Days

This measure looks at how good the business is at getting paid for its efforts. It determines the number of days from the date of invoicing before getting paid. The larger the number, the slower customers are to pay. The debtor days ratio is calculated as follows:

- **Debtor Days** = Debtors/(Sales/365).

Debtor days represents the average collection period. In simple terms, if the debtor days ratio is high, the business is financing its customers' businesses, by providing its own money to help them to do business. Even worse, it could be borrowing money from a bank to finance its customers' businesses.

The use of Pareto analysis is recommended on debtors. Are all customers slow to pay, or is there a clearly identifiable core of slow payers? If such a 'slow core' can be identified, then the challenge facing the business is to find a way either to redress this situation or to find replacement customers. The alternative – a costly one – is to continue to provide a quasi-banking service to its customers. If the problem is because of poor systems in the accounts area, then this is an issue to be tackled internally.

The introduction of debtor days as a management metric often can result, in and of itself, an improvement in performance in this centrally important area.

Creditor Days

The balance to debtor days is creditor days. This is a measure of the time it takes you to pay your suppliers and is calculated as follows:

- **Creditor Days** = Creditors/(Purchases/365).

By paying creditors on time, one can usually expect – and even demand – a good service level. If a business gets a reputation as a poor payer, then it becomes very difficult to expect good service or help and support with supplier development activities.

Supermarkets' customers pay on receipt of goods while their creditors deliver at short notice and on 30+ day terms of payment. A well-run supermarket can make significant contribution to profit based on this margin between money coming in and money going out.

The challenge for businesses generally is to close the gap between debtors and creditors days ratios, to recognise cash as an asset, and to manage this asset effectively. If the creditor days figure is lower than debtor days, then your business is financing your customers' businesses. A fine balancing act needs to take place between these two ratios. The closer the ratios are and the lower the absolute number for each, the better the situation.

Other Key Operational Ratios

A number of other financial ratios can be very useful to the non-financial manager:

- Sales or Turnover Growth;
- Wages or Direct Labour Growth;
- Materials Purchase Growth;
- Overhead Growth;
- Debtors to Revenue Growth;
- Creditors to Revenue Growth;
- Net Assets Growth.

The key factor with all these ratios is the change in the measure over time. If wages are growing faster than turnover, there may be a problem. Similarly for the other metrics.

These metrics are relatively easy to capture and to track over time. Their use can be very helpful in the early identification of problems within a business.

FINANCIER'S RATIOS

The ratios discussed so far are of an operational nature – they can help a manager to run his or her business in an effective way. There also are a number of measures that are often used by financial institutions or investors if they are examining a business. It is worthwhile for a manager to be aware of these measures to understand how a bank, external agency or potential investor will examine your business based on its financial data.

Return on Net Assets (RONA)

RONA examines how effective a business is at generating wealth, a return on the investment made. It is calculated as follows:

- **RONA** = (Profit Before Interest & Taxes) Net Assets.

The key to the use of RONA as a measure is to examine the cost of debt *versus* the RONA metric being recorded. If a company borrows capital at, say, 10% and its RONA figure is 15%, then there is a positive margin of 5%. If the business has a RONA figure of less than 10%, its cost of capital, then it is effectively borrowing capital to lose it. In many businesses, RONA can be below the cost of capital in the general market. In such cases, if it were possible, the business would be better served to liquidate and to invest the money in the capital markets.

Interest Cover

One of the first checks done by a prospective lender is on the level of interest cover. This is a simple calculation that examines the ability of the business to cover its debt payments and is calculated as:

- (Interest Costs & Earnings before extraordinary items) x 100
  Interest Costs

At its most basic level, the ratio should be over 100. If the ratio is less than 100, the business will be unable to meet its debt payments; at 100, it is just able to meet them. In normal circumstances, an analyst will look for a ratio of 300 to 400 when analysing a company's accounts.

Liquidity Ratio

There are two liquidity ratios in general use:

- Current ratio;
- Acid Test ratio.

These liquidity ratios examine a business' ability to meet its current liabilities. The ratios are calculated as follows:

- **Current ratio** = (Current Assets) / (Current Liabilities);
- **Acid Test ratio** = (Current Assets – Stock) / (Current Liabilities).

In general, the acid test ratio is more severe than the current ratio. Analysts typically look for a ratio of 1 or greater for this metric. The current ratio is usually targeted at 2 or greater. Specific sector and market norms are very important when using these liquidity ratios.

ACTIVITY BASED COSTING

Activity Based Costing seeks to help management to understand the real costs associated with making a product or providing a service. Many costing systems allocate the general business overhead on an arbitrary basis – by number of employees, per square metre of floor space occupied or some other similarly arbitrary measure.

Activity Based Costing seeks to allocate true costs to specific activities within an operation, based on the actual usage of resources. Using Activity Based Costing, a complicated, poor-performing computer system that needs regular attention would have a higher percentage of the IT Department costs allocated to it than a more reliable system.

Activity Based Costing looks at costs at four different levels:

- **Unit:** Direct costs such as labour and materials and also activity-specific costs such as electricity and machine financing;

- **Batch:** Costs directly attributable to processing a batch such as set-up time, inspection costs, paper handling and complaints;

- **Product / Process:** Items such as maintenance costs on machinery, changes to the service requiring engineering input, and service development costs.

- **Organisation:** Business level costs related to staying in business such as depreciation, staff costs in administration, marketing and other functional departments.

The Activity Based Costing approach provides management with specific and focused insight into what is happening in an operation and where the money flows are. Decisions become based on detailed facts rather than opinion or very high-level information. Experience has shown that the application of LB techniques, in conjunction with the Activity Based Costing approach, often highlights the fact that products that seemed to be loss leaders can be developed into real stars.

Finally, remember that the cost of providing a service does not determine what the selling price should be. Selling price is most usually defined by competition, a market's ability or inclination to absorb a specific price level and by a business' aggression in that market. The use of Activity Based Costing, Lean Business and Benchmarking practices can help a business to be more aggressive, as it moves to becoming more capable, rather than having to give away margin in order to gain sales.

CONCLUSION

Financial analysis is a demanding and often quite sophisticated area of endeavour. The basic tools presented here can help a non-financial manager to understand some aspects of their business from the point of view of a financial person.

The use of selected key metrics can help to bring objectivity to an operation and can provide an early warning to a management team of a change in circumstances. If managers are tuned to be aware of these changes, then they can take action to address them before serious issues develop.

These ratios need to be treated with caution and used carefully. No single measure can tell the full story of a business and they are most useful when used to map trends over time.

15: Supply Chain & Logistics

A company does not exist in a vacuum. Most companies are part of a supply chain, either relying on others to supply them with goods or services or supplying their services to others who rely on them. Many Irish software companies provide services and supports to many of the world's leading companies, seamlessly and invisibly to the end customer. An analysis of the leading companies in the world has shown that up to 85% of the cost of their products is bought in from other suppliers. So far, we have focused on building capability and effectiveness within a business. Now, let's look at the supply chain.

A number of service companies have made significant business opportunities out of the supply chain process itself. Such world-leading companies as DHL and local logistics leaders Nightline have created business models that have evolved to meet the dynamic needs of customers.

DHL, once a postal delivery company, has now developed business elements that include delivery of post but also the provision of outsourced logistics services to major manufacturing companies. DHL provides an aggregation service for suppliers to such companies as Land Rover. It acts as the receiving warehouse for parts suppliers. It then manages the parts, ensuring just-in-time deliveries to the assembly plant. This model of outsourced materials management – effectively logistics as an integrated service – is being adopted in many of the world's leading automotive and manufacturing companies. The prime manufacturers realise that managing logistics is not a core competence and so they have called on logistics experts to provide this service.

Nightline has evolved from a pure parcel delivery company into a full logistics company. Its recent development of ParcelMotel came from an analysis of the evolved needs of customers, where the increase in online sales through the Internet has led to the requirement for personalised 'last mile' delivery systems. The company identified that there were many instances where the final delivery could not take place due to people not being at their home address during business hours so it developed a drop-off location where items could be delivered and collected by the consumer, at their leisure. The company also identified a further opportunity, through the free delivery offered by major e-sales companies to addresses in the UK compared to the high shipping rates charged to addresses in Ireland. By allowing its customers to use an address in Northern Ireland and then trans-shipping their purchases to a delivery location close to their home, ParcelMotel can offer Irish customers a lower overall delivery cost. Creativity and innovation also has a place in the logistics and service provision area, based on customers' spoken and unspoken needs.

Realising that a business is part of a supply chain helps you to understand the complexity of the business. You have already identified wastes in administration, product development, sales and distribution areas; now let's look for similar wastes in internal materials management and planning areas as well as with, and between, suppliers. The marketplace today demands short lead times and high levels of flexibility. A business can meet these demands either by having large amounts of systems and resource redundancy, just in case, or by holding large stock levels of finished goods and raw materials or by developing both internal capabilities and its relationships with its suppliers.

A business must identify suppliers who:

- Can and do meet its requirements for superior service;
- Could develop to meet these needs;
- Will not or cannot meet these needs.

Big and small businesses rely on supply chains for survival and growth. Like many other aspects of a Lean Business approach, until focus is brought on to the facts relating to suppliers and the interactions with them, opinions will abound. Many companies continue to do business with poor quality suppliers over many years, because they often feel they have no choice. In many cases, they do have choices, just they do not seem to understand that they can take them.

Over the past 10 years, many larger companies have moved to develop their suppliers. They have taken the time to transfer technologies and understanding to them. In many cases, staff from the bigger companies effectively have mentored the smaller companies. This transfer of knowledge and understanding was not done for any altruistic reason but for purely business ones. The bigger companies are moving up the value chain, seeking to add value to their services and products through high level design, system integration and customer service rather than through performing basic manufacturing operations. Apple is an extreme example. The company has moved from being a computer maker to being a lifestyle company, where its products and services such as the iPhone and iTunes are seamlessly integrated into people's lives, providing solutions to problems that in many cases the consumer did not know they had.

Leading companies also have come to rely on smaller companies to provide expertise and innovation in particular aspects of their products. Many Irish companies have developed expertise in areas such as finance, telecoms, education and gaming that provide solutions to the big companies for parts of their businesses that are necessary but not core technologies for them. In a number of cases, the technologies developed by Irish companies underpin the core products of the leading companies. This transfer of responsibility to smaller companies has proven very beneficial for the companies that have risen to the challenge, and very difficult for those who have not. The arrangement along the supply chain is like a pyramid, as in **Figure 15.1**.

FIGURE 15.1: THE SUPPLY CHAIN

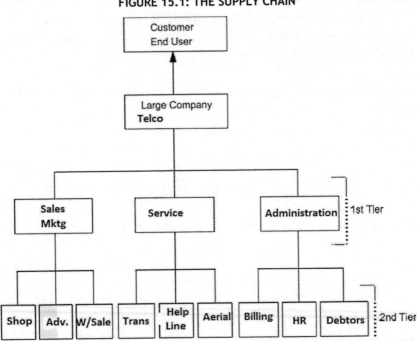

A telco company deals with the customer or end-user and focuses its attention on understanding its customer's needs and dealing with them in an effective way. It can decide to outsource many of the functions of the business to external service providers, upon whom it depends for major elements of its service. It also depends on these suppliers for levels of innovation in their particular areas of expertise. For the pyramid to work, it is clear that all levels need to be working to the same standard, with similar objectives. It would be totally inappropriate to have a low-quality second-tier company working for a high-quality first-tier or end-user company.

The supply chain is simply a strand of the pyramid. Now let's look at some of the key aspects of supply chain and how it relates to small and medium-sized companies.

PURCHASING – IS PRICE KING?

How many suppliers service your business? Are purchases made based on price, at a quality level of course? Or are such things as variety, service, flexibility, delivery and innovative ability taken into consideration?

By buying only on the basis of price, businesses often miss the opportunity to secure real competitive advantage. Currently, Indian, Eastern European and Far Eastern service providers are cheaper on price for a number of services, at least when price alone is considered. Factor in language difficulties, potential quality problems, lack of local understanding, loss of corporate image and a reduction in knowledge from one-to-one contact with customers and the cost advantages of outsourcing quickly can become negative. Would it be possible to develop a relationship with a local supplier, where the hidden costs of doing business between companies could be identified and removed, and which in turn would result in lower true pricing while retaining the competitive advantages that close proximity, flexibility and responsiveness can bring?

The key here is 'working together'. If companies and suppliers can examine the purchasing process and the paper trail associated with it, from initial request for quotation to payment and credit note procedures, and can simplify the process, they often can remove wastes, thereby reducing costs, while retaining local supply with all the benefits that that brings in terms of understanding, responsiveness and flexibility. Such relationships need to be based on trust, between both parties, so that savings realised along the chain can be shared and help to derive further savings.

But price alone is not king. Some companies have created positions for themselves at the tops of pyramids, others populate the sides and foundation levels. Companies such as Apple, Vodafone, the banks, and others depend on their suppliers to create innovations in the systems they supply to their customers. The supplier is given broad performance, cost and quality parameters and then can innovate within those boundaries. Small companies often tend to be very good at their specific business. They know a lot about the technologies they use, the processes they apply and how to maximise performance from their limited resources. Big companies rely on these abilities, and often can help small companies to understand and use systems to help them meet ever-increasing standards of quality and service. By working together, the full supply chain can benefit.

QUICKER, BETTER, CHEAPER ... TOGETHER

The pressure is on for business to perform at higher levels of ability. Customers demand better and better service, delivered quicker and at better perceived quality levels. Much of the Lean Service approach to date has focused on what can be done within your own business to be better. Now let's look at the 'Together' element of Lean Service – what you, with your suppliers and business service partners, can do to help deliver superior value to your customers at least effort.

Many service businesses exist based on superior knowledge: of a technology, a skill, or legislation or a tax code or a data set. Engineering supply businesses are fundamentally a warehousing operation but their key differentiating factor is that they know where to get things. They have knowledge, based around a supply base that makes it easier for their customers to source materials from them rather than find those sources themselves. These supply businesses charge a premium for this knowledge. Wholesalers in general act as a sourcing service. Through their identification of market-appropriate suppliers, they act as middlemen between producers, retailers and consumers. Many of the Lean Service tools relating to sales, visualisation and check sheets are very suitable for a warehousing operator that is trying to meet the needs of intermediary shops, which in turn are hoping to meet the needs of consumers. The 'steps of remove', where the producer deals through the wholesaler / distributor, through the store to the consumer can lead to major challenges in ensuring that the market gets satisfied while enabling each of the key actors to make a living. This requires the key actors to understand the nature of the chain and also to look for ways to optimise value retention along it.

The choices made as to how a business is organised will affect fundamentally its ability to deliver. If a business is set up, structured and resourced to constantly seek to optimise its supply chain, it has a good opportunity to do so. And it is more likely to retain value than one that is not looking to get better.

If you think creatively when arranging facilities, offices, manufacturing, or design departments, materials stores and feedback and management systems, you can find ways to build in flexibility, to remove time wastage and to ensure delivery of a quality service to customers.

Identifying which are good suppliers, who has the potential and the will to grow and who is willing to tackle inter-business wastes, is a major start toward to securing increased competitiveness.

GETTING CLOSE

The demands of the marketplace mean business needs to be agile, responsive, and quality conscious. The previous section mentioned the 'steps of remove', that is the number of intermediary steps between producer, their suppliers and the consumer. A big challenge in a Lean Service environment is to shorten the time along the supply chain, so that you can service your customers without them seeing any appreciable time delay. In the early days of Lean implementation, the supply chain stretched from the manufacturer to the supplier, as in **Figure 15.2**.

FIGURE 15.2: THE SUPPLY CHAIN 1

Manufacturer	- Low inventory
	- Stable production
Supplier	- High inventory
	- Pressure situation, poor visibility

At that time, 'just-in-time' meant that the big company held very little stock and demanded that their suppliers held it for them. The links with customers or end-users were often very poor. As the market changed, and the understanding of the possibilities of world-class practices developed, the importance of top class communication became clearer, as shown in **Figure 15.3**.

FIGURE 15.3: THE SUPPLY CHAIN 2

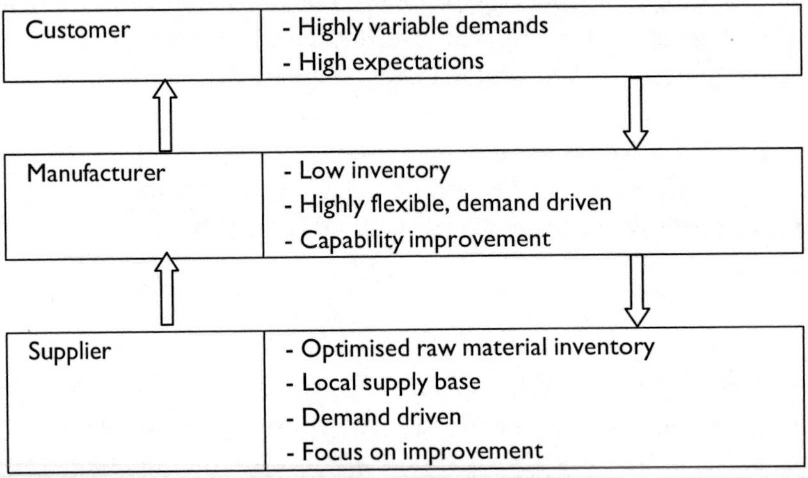

Customer	- Highly variable demands - High expectations
Manufacturer	- Low inventory - Highly flexible, demand driven - Capability improvement
Supplier	- Optimised raw material inventory - Local supply base - Demand driven - Focus on improvement

Developments in web technology and customer needs analysis tools led to the development of effective communication systems along the supply chain, as in **Figure 15.4**.

By focusing on building capability in the manufacturer, the supplier and the intermediary stock holders, the levels of stock and the time to deliver to the customer both can be reduced.

A balance needs to be struck between the use of computer systems and data transfer as aids to meeting customer needs and as internal management tools. Has a picture of the purchasing patterns of key customers been created? Do they have a purchasing pattern? If a pattern can be identified, it is often possible to communicate this to the customer to optimise the supply of materials along the supply chain. Some businesses are unaware of the impact of their purchasing patterns on their own businesses, let alone on others.

FIGURE 15.4: DATA LINKS ALONG THE SUPPLY CHAIN

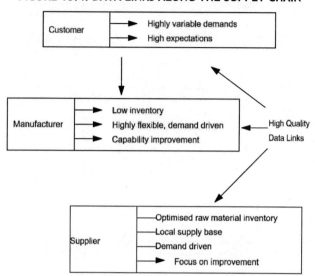

An example of two purchasing patterns are shown in **Figure 15.5**. The first pattern was the 'normal' pattern of the customer: order a large quantity of product, use the product until it runs out and then pressure the wholesaler for rapid re-supply of another large quantity of stock.

When stocks ran out, production of their own products was delayed, which led to increased overtime being worked after the deliveries were received and unnecessary delays in providing service to their customers. When the wholesaler mapped out this pattern of purchasing, a revised order pattern was developed, resulting in no stock shortages, reduced inventory costs and significantly reduced overtime charges, expedition charges and reduced pressure on the business.

Once again, do customers have a purchasing pattern? How can they be helped to see this pattern and to develop a new pattern that suits both wholesaler and customer businesses?

FIGURE 15.5: PURCHASING PATTERNS

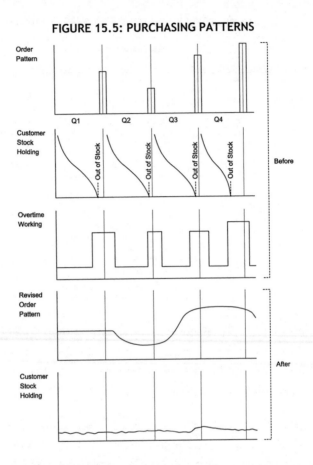

STOCK ANALYSIS & MANAGEMENT

The most expensive component in any product is the one that is out of stock when it is needed. The real role of stock management is to ensure that parts and components are available to operations, as they are needed. The difficult balancing act of stock management is to achieve this objective with a minimum of stock holding.

The traditional approach to stock management has been to introduce paper-based or computer-based stock control programmes. Stocks of parts are listed and checked and issued to production. The effectiveness of the system is dependent on the accuracy of paperwork within the system and the conscientiousness of all involved. For such systems to be reliable, accuracy levels of over 95%

are required. Each of these stock checks and paper transactions adds cost to the part, but no value. The focus in a Lean environment is to find ways to maximise the value, while minimising the cost and providing effective management to the business.

For example, on a recent visit by one of the authors to Subaru Cars in Japan, the number of exhaust manifolds sitting beside the assembly line was counted. A quick mental calculation, based on Subaru's daily throughput of cars, suggested that it had only two hours' worth of exhaust manifolds at the line. There was another two hours' worth in stores. This is in stark contrast to Western manufacturers, where days – if not weeks' – worth of parts and components are kept in store. A visit to Scania Trucks a number of years ago showed that it had invested heavily in installing a fully automated storage and retrieval system for completed engines, giving it one week's stock.

By the way, the calculations made earlier in relation to Subaru were wrong. The type of engine in the Subaru is known as a boxer engine, a horizontally-opposed flat-four engine, in which two exhaust manifolds are used per car. So Subaru was only stocking one hour's worth of manifolds! Its suppliers were delivering manifolds continually during each day.

Practical Stock Management – ABC Analysis

To reduce the cost of stocking items, one needs to understand how the cost is made up. Not all items are equally costly, not all items are sold in the same volume. Before one can decide on the best management policy for items, one needs to know which items must be managed. Again, simple ABC analysis can help in this regard.

The process starts with a listing of the items in the stores. This list is augmented with the annual usage levels and item unit price. Annual usage value is then calculated:

- **Annual Usage Value** = Annual Usage x Unit Cost.

The list of items is then sorted by annual usage value. Based on the Pareto principle, approximately 20% of the items will be responsible for 80% of the annual spend. This first 20% of items are known as the A class items.

These A class items need to be managed aggressively. If possible, they should be located in a special area of the stores or, better still, where this is feasible, directly at the point of usage. In any case, the gathering of the A class items into one area helps focus attention on these costly items. Every effort should be made to develop supplier relationships to minimise the level of these stocks that need to be maintained. In many cases, suppliers can accommodate requirements for more frequent deliveries if asked, and also if they are given some visibility on annual usage levels.

The focus of attention on an item's usage also should extend to looking at suppliers for items. Are there many suppliers for the same item? Is there a good, still valid reason for this? Or is it just the way things are? Quite often, such purchasing patterns develop over time. The ABC analysis process can highlight these issues and possibly provide an opportunity to rationalise the supplier list, aggregate purchases with a core of suppliers and thus achieve improved terms of business.

B class items also can be identified from the annual usage value list – usually, they account for 15% or so of annual purchases. These items warrant less management input and can most readily be managed on, say, a two-weekly or monthly Kanban system.

C class items usually account for the last 5% of the annual usage and are the least important, from a financial point of view. However, the smallest, cheapest item can be the most costly, especially if it is out of stock and a customer decides to go elsewhere where they can get a 'full set'. C class items do not need to be managed aggressively – but a Kanban of three months' usage levels should ensure sufficient items are held in stock with minimal management input.

The availability of items to operations or sales staff in an efficient manner should be the objective of procurement staff. This can best be achieved through the development of both internal systems and a well- tuned, committed and capable supply chain.

LEAN CLUSTERS

There is strength in unity. Small and medium-sized companies have certain advantages and disadvantages when compared to large, multi-national type companies.

FIGURE 15.6: ADVANTAGES & DISADVANTAGES OF SMES

Advantages	Disadvantages
Flexible	Short of people
Quick to move	Dependent on key player
Short lines of	Small scale
communication	Limited scope

Imagine if a number of SMEs were to align themselves into a virtual organisation, where their respective strengths would work together to build scale, address the people shortages and make the whole virtual organisation less dependent on individuals.

This approach is followed in a number of leading areas of the business world, most notably in the major consultancy, legal and accountancy firms. Many of these organisations are groupings of professionals where partners are just that, partners who decide to work collectively to achieve the benefits of scale and to be able to offer 'full service' offerings to clients.

By specialising in their own areas, they can develop true ability and expertise, and by co-operating, they can provide services to Lean standards, competitively.

This approach is dependent on high levels of communication and trust between companies. The linking of companies in this way ensures the mobility of small companies, the retention of their key advantages and the creation of the 'virtual scale' necessary to facilitate competition in the international market place.

The application of Lean Business techniques between companies clustering can lead to the identification and eradication of wastes. We have seen how these tools and techniques can do this within an individual business, but the opportunity also exists to develop an approach for Irish SMEs to apply Lean Business techniques in a cluster approach.

Case Study 6: Thornton Partners

As property insurance loss adjusters, we investigate and manage to conclusion property insurance claims on behalf of insurers. Loss adjusting requires a field inspection of damage and evaluation of the cause and cost. The process requires the loss adjuster to report to the client insurer, to maintain contact with the policyholder and to finalise the claim. We are subject to regulation by the Central Bank of Ireland (CBI) and to regular audit by our clients for conformance to quality standards and cost management.

Our new instructions from clients had reduced – from 880 per month for the previous financial year to 650 per month in the current year – representing a significant loss of income and resulting in some staff redundancies. Bluntly, our operations had a problem with quality.

When I examined how claims were assigned to our loss adjusters, I found that every claim was treated the same, irrespective of value, complexity or the loss adjuster's experience or competence. Claims were assigned according to geographical and availability criteria, meaning that often less experienced adjusters were handling high value/ complex losses.

The objectives for my initiative were to improve the quality of our service-product to clients.

Early discussions persuaded me to focus on the external drivers for change and to present these in ways that senior managers could understand and relate to. I posited the idea that the Central Bank of Ireland (CBI), a body whose requirement for compliance was total, could be used as an external driver and that documents issuing from CBI could be interpreted to comprise and support a quality improvement objective. I developed a 13-point Compliance template that set out all of the performance indicators that could arguably be seen as being compliance-related but which were more appropriately business performance objectives. I also established a Quality Strategy Group (QSG) comprising employees across the business being brought together to learn process improvement techniques and to discuss business problems.

Prior to my initiative, we had one performance indicator report, known as the operations report. However, this report, produced weekly, contained only the following:

- Number of new claims;
- To whom they were assigned;
- Those cases that had closed;
- Fee income generated.

It did not measure our compliance with the CBI's requirements nor did it measure our performance in terms of quality (effectively, conformance with client requirements).

We held a process-mapping workshop with five of our loss adjusters and asked them to:

- Identify the key performance objectives for the process;
- Write out each activity on each stage of the process;
- Validate with others outside the group;
- Start the process again.

We then asked our IT development specialist to join the group and to help us identify opportunities for using technology.

' Seeing first', we all imagined how the appointments, inspection and reporting elements of our process would work best. This creative work allowed us to develop a series of iterations over a number of months that ended in a business process that produced compliance with our service-level agreements with clients in respect of contact with their customers following our instruction; inspection of the claim; issuance of 'compliance letter' from the site; production of our preliminary report for our client from the site plus uploading of key information to our mainframe system; a quality assurance check day one – and all within 72 hours of our instruction by the client without any extra work.

The performance measurement system that I introduced now reports on other measures of quality that are assessed by our clients, including:

- Number of new cases assigned per adjuster/ per team;
- Number of cases finalised per week/ month;
- Average cost per claim;
- Proportion of cases where liability was declined;
- Number of cases where a decision on liability is outstanding so that the manager can intervene and support the adjuster to make a decision;
- Number of cases per adjuster outstanding;

- Percentage of cases where preliminary report issued to client within 48 hours of inspection;
- Percentage of cases where final report issued within 24 hours of agreement of claim;
- Average life-cycle per claim, per adjuster and variance from the organisation average.

A second performance measurement report measures other variables in the life-cycle of a claim for the whole business:

- Time taken to make initial contact with policyholder;
- Time taken to inspect case;
- Percentage of cases where liability confirmation ('compliance') letters have been issued;
- Percentage of cases where preliminary report has been issued to client within 48 hours of inspection.

However, whilst quantitative measures of quality are assessed, certain aspects of the claim life-cycle were more qualitative and were difficult to measure and report on:

- The adjuster's evaluation of the loss on site;
- The adjuster's evaluation of the policyholder's claim submission fairly and within five business days;
- The standard of narrative used by the adjuster in correspondence and reports.

Nonetheless, the fruits of this work were that, over six months of iteration and piloting, we developed a process technology that helped us achieve just over 95% compliance with certain performance indicators set by our clients and up from 47% when we started.

16: Innovation & Design

Most Lean companies are trying to do two things simultaneously:

- Continuously improving existing services and systems, with the objective of getting better at what they are currently doing;

- Searching for a breakthrough, to enter new markets by developing new services or processes and to change their position in existing markets by doing different things from what they are currently doing.

The orientation of Lean companies is to continuously 're-invent the company' – a form of accelerated Darwinian evolution of the company. Re-invention is a process of taking advantage of such environmental changes as markets, technology, politics and changing lifestyles. Exploiting new markets and new opportunities as quickly as possible is a crucial success factor. The concept of re-inventing the company is at variance with the idea, which was popular in the 1980s, of creating and maintaining long-term competitive advantage – an unsustainable approach in the hyper-competitive 2000s.

Consider the following quotations:

- **From Peters (1987):** "Operations must become a, if not *the*, primary marketing tool in the firm's arsenal. Quality, maintainability, responsiveness … flexibility, and the length of the innovation cycle (for both incremental improvement of current services and major new service development) are all controlled by the business";

- **From Kenney and Florida (1993):** "The operation is no longer a place of noisy work stations and people doing repetitive things, but rather an environment of on-going experimentation and continuous innovation".

INNOVATION

Research workers use resources in seeking fundamental knowledge and understanding of 'what is', whereas development workers use resources and research findings to create for the market 'what never has been'.

Innovation is closer to development work than to research work, is generally associated with wealth creation, and includes:

- New service development;
- Process development;
- Management practices development;
- Business model development.

New service development and process development will be considered below in the section on Design.

Management practices development is concerned with the development and adaptation of different management practices with a view to increasing the overall productivity of the organisation. The use of soft skills can have a profound impact on competitiveness. Soft skills here include:

- Methods of organisation;
- Methods of working;
- Managerial philosophy;
- Leadership style;
- Communications;
- Supplier relationships.

The objective for the organisation is to work better or more effectively rather than more intensively.

Business model development is innovation in relation to the manner the company conducts its business. With the advent of e-business, in its different forms, companies now have opportunities of creating and serving global markets in ways that were not available some years ago. It is now possible to consider the development of 'virtual organisations' to service specific markets and to form temporary alliances for some projects with organisations with whom one is competing with on other projects.

DESIGN

New Service Development

The basic purpose of any business organisation is to provide services to satisfy the requirements of its customers. Customers may independently specify their requirements and / or may be conditioned / educated to request certain characteristics of services provided by the organisation. The requirements of customers are fundamental inputs to strategy formulation for the organisation. New service development (NSD) is often considered to be an essential ingredient for the long-term survival of a business. Some commentators even consider NSD to be the *raison d'être* of a business.

Process and service design can confer competitive advantage on any organisation, either through cost leadership or service differentiation. Appropriate design is a key to superior performance, no matter which mode of competition the organisation follows.

The two main two types of design are:

- **Service design:** Concerned with the specification of the physical items, together with the sensual and psychological benefits the customer receives from the service experience;

- **Process design:** Concerned with the specification of the processes by which the service is delivered. In the provision of services, the customer is often an integral part of the service provided and so process design, in this case, also must consider issues relating to the convenience and comfort of the customer, the demeanour and approach of the server and the physical environment in which the service is delivered.

There is a very close relationship between good design of a service and the perceived quality of that service. Quality is essentially concerned with meeting or exceeding customers' expectations. The design function defines an organisation more clearly than other functions, in that it builds on the core competencies of the organisation and exposes gaps where new competencies must be established. Uniquely, design simultaneously specifies the customers of the organisation as well as its competitors.

Good design therefore should achieve:

- A close match between service offerings and customer requirements;
- A cost-effective and timely achievement of these requirements;
- A process that leads to ease of delivery of service.

In addition, speed of delivery of completed designs of new services is a very significant competitive advantage. A study undertaken by McKinsey & Co found:

- A 50% overrun in development costs affects profits by 35%;
- Service delivery costs that are 9% too high have a 22% impact on profitability;
- Shipping an offering to market six months too late leads to a 33% deterioration in total profits.

The key point is that design has a very serious impact on an organisation's profitability.

Design as a Process rather than a Function

It's obvious that service businesses are in existence to create, make and market services. Many organisations, and particularly SMEs, however, tend to be involved in either mainly the production of products or mainly the delivery of a service, but not usually both.

The design process begins with ideas for new or improved services. The sources for these ideas are many, including the organisation's own staff, marketing research, customer complaints and suggestions, suppliers, new service offerings developed by competitors, developments in new technology and services designed for markets other than your usual markets. Cultivating an 'innovative outlook' within an organisation is a characteristic of Lean business. To develop such a culture, employees must feel valued and be encouraged to express their views and make suggestions for improvements. Tolerance of failure, to some degree at least, is an essential element in the development of such a culture. Not all suggestions or ideas for innovation will be fruitful, but the cost of missing out on the one that would be fruitful could be very high. Needless to say, a balance must be struck between the resources devoted to innovation and new idea generation and the normal expected day-to-day work of the organisation.

Given the business paradigm of Create – Make – Market – Assess, or the analogous Plan – Do – Check – Act cycle (PDCA - Deming Wheel) for continuous improvement, it is clear that product design is a multi- disciplinary process.

FIGURE 16.1: THE PDCA CYCLE

ASSESS Information from Market Place	CREATE Idea Generation Design of Product	ACT Full implementation Continue the improvement cycle	PLAN Problem Identification and Plan for Improvement
MARKET Sales	MAKE Manufacture Buy in Parts	CHECK/STUDY Results of Implementation	DO Implementation on a pilot basis

CMMA Cycle	PDCA Cycle
Produce Cycle	The Deming Wheel

However, in addition to being multi-disciplinary, best practice in service design is that the disciplines / departments work together on the design concurrently, and not sequentially, or 'over the wall', as tended to be the practice in the past. Concurrent design / simultaneous development is a prerequisite for reducing the time-to-market of new services.

It is well-known that failure rates in new services development and introductions to the market are high, but these rates may be reduced by a company-wide multi-functional, rather than a single-function, approach to new services innovation. New service offering development is a key opportunity for organisational learning, either through the development of technology or by forming alliances with other companies.

FIGURE 16.2: DEPARTMENTAL WALLS

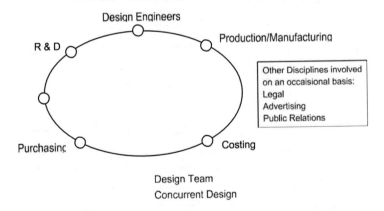

FIGURE 16.3: MULTI-FUNCTIONAL TEAMS

A major push today focuses on Lean Service development, where ideas are trialled quickly and cheaply to determine market receptivity rather than ploughing ahead with a new service only to find that the market doesn't want it. This approach is being championed in the software sector.

The advantage of using multi-disciplinary design teams in a concurrent fashion are two-fold: cost and speed. Any required changes in the design of a service become much more costly the closer the service is to release time to market. If a service design has to be changed during delivery (resulting in lots of changes), the cost can be very high and might have been avoided, or reduced substantially, if operations personnel had been involved with the design at an earlier stage. Likewise, it is important that marketing stays with the design team until delivery, and even after delivery, to ensure that customers' requirements are met.

There are clear quality advantages in operations being involved with the service design from the beginning because, as is well-known, quality thrives in a stable environment from an operations viewpoint. The fewer changes the better from the point of view of operations, once service delivery starts.

Techniques that may be of benefit in developing ideas for new services include:

- **Brainstorming**, which is a group technique for the identification and solution of problems. It is essential to have free expression of ideas and no criticism of any idea presented. Ideas are evaluated only *after* the completion of the brainstorming session. Brainstorming may be used in other areas, including quality improvement and process change;

- **Benchmarking**, itself, is clearly a source of new product ideas. Finding the best in class service or process and measuring the performance of the organisation against such standards is often a very important source of new ideas for services and processes;

- **Perceptual maps** are visual displays comparing customer perceptions of different service offerings (**Figure 16.4** presents a perceptual map of a particular meal in a specified price range. There is clearly a market in this price range for a good taste, good ambience meal!);

- **Reverse Engineering** involves carefully studying and inspecting the services of competitors to assess design features. Such features can be adapted or enhanced, thus avoiding any patent infringement.

FIGURE 16.4: PERCEPTUAL MAPS

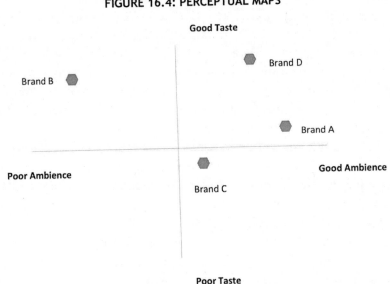

Very few SMEs can afford the costs and risks associated with large R&D departments, since ideas generated by R&D often follow a very long path to commercialisation. Moreover, only about 5% of ideas for services are translated into actual services in the market place.

SMEs can use consultancy help from outside organisations. However, to obtain full benefit from such assistance, the SME must remain involved with the outside consultant and there should be a very clear focus on what is expected from the consultant. Institutes of Technology and universities may be of assistance in some aspects of design but, again, such assistance must be managed properly for maximum benefit. Remember that, whereas the consultant receives the fee, the company takes the risk in the marketplace.

Once the idea for a new service has been generated, the design process can commence. There are distinct phases in the design process as indicated in **Figure 16.5**.

FIGURE 16.5: DESIGN PROCESS PHASES

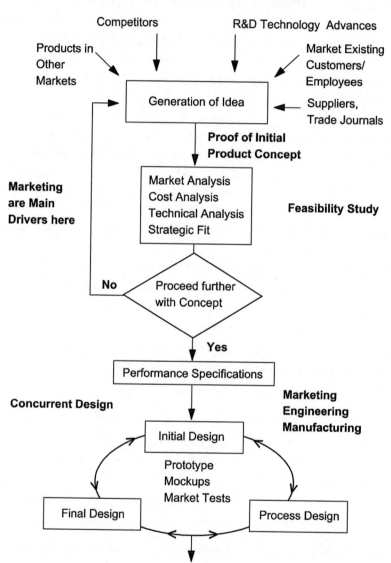

PRODUCT DESIGN & MANUFACTURING PROCESS SPECIFICATIONS

In the feasibility study, or proof of initial service concept, phase, alternative concepts are evaluated using some form of market research such as customer surveys, focus groups, interviews and discussions with experienced sales personnel. If there is a perceived demand for the new service, then initial cost analysis should be undertaken.

Technologies such as break-even analysis, decision theory, discounted cash flow are sometimes used to evaluate the profitability of providing the service. Data used in most cost analyses are probabilistic rather than certain in nature and so any such analysis should include an assessment of the risk involved and, consequently, the organisation's attitude to risk. Associated with the cost analysis, there is a need to consider technical and strategic issues relating to the proposed new service.

The following questions must be answered:

- Does the organisation have the managerial and technical skill required to manage the new service development project and actually provide the service?
- Are there any capital resources requirements that the organisation may have difficulty in funding?
- Is the overall risk excessive?
- What about available or unused capacity in operational areas?
- Are there likely to be any supplier problems?
- Is there a good strategic fit with other offerings currently being delivered?
- Is the new service offering compatible with the core business of the company and will it provide competitive advantage?

Clearly, the input of top management is very desirable, before it is decided to proceed with the detail design of the service. Arising out of the feasibility study, performance specifications for the new service can be developed, describing what the service offering should do to satisfy customer requirements.

Once this stage is reached, the philosophy of full concurrent design comes into play. The performance specifications are translated into technical specifications of the service. An initial design is developed, a prototype is developed, the prototype is tested in the market and a further design is developed. The sequence of design – build a prototype – test – redesign – may be repeated a number of times until the design team is satisfied. The concept of Minimum Viable Offering is once again to the fore here. As ideas are developed they can be trialled with customers to see whether the company has met the requirements of the customer and also whether the customer values their offering, before excessive investment is made in time and resources. Software often goes through alpha and beta testing with good customers and 'super-users', while food products are often panel-tested.

Note that service design includes both form design and function design:

- **Form Design**: Concerned with the appearance of the service, what the customer sees, style and the experience of the service. Image, personal identification and market appeal are all part of form design. Form design may be very important for consumer products – for example, on-line gaming, trading, sharing – but less so in industrial services – for example, motor generator sets, tax management;

- **Function Design**: Concerned with how the service performs. In some services, form design usually takes precedence over function design. However, function design ensures the service's fitness for use by the customer. Two important criteria of function design are the reliability and maintainability of the service after delivery – no one wants their on-line files or data to be lost or made available to people who shouldn't have access them.

The process design goes hand in hand with the service design, and the whole design process is one of iteration to an end position of final service design and final process design, both of which are taken over by the operations team for implementation.

Lean organisations are assisted during the design process by the use of techniques such as quality function deployment (QFD), CAD / CAM, computer-aided process planning (CAPP), failure mode effects analysis (FMEA), fault tree analysis (FTA) and value analysis (VA).

Design teams should keep in mind the need to protect the company against liability claims. The best defence against such claims are design reviews with a comprehensive and defendable trail of state-of-the-art design decisions taken in respect of the service. After the delivery process has settled down, various quality assurance techniques are required to optimise quality objectives.

Now let's look at a number of specific elements of design that can contribute significantly to both cost and quality of delivered services, in a simple way, including:

- Simultaneous design;
- Design for delivery;
- Modularity;
- Standardisation;
- Code count;
- Design for testing;
- Design for process;
- Product evaluation.

Simultaneous Development

Simultaneous development can work where communication levels are good. The traditional design process results in sequential development. Designs are completed before packaging work starts, before operations processes are designed, before materials are sourced, etc. This results in a build-up of lead-times, as each downstream department has its own lead-time requirements to complete the specific stages of the new service introduction process.

By ensuring that communication levels are good, individual team members can make decisions that short-circuit the overall service introduction cycle. Design and marketing need to work closely together so that designers truly understand the needs and desires of the end-users. As this closeness develops, a company's services are more closely attuned to the requirements of the marketplace and so are more likely to be bought.

Design for Delivery

A well-designed service with lots of marketable features that cannot be delivered effectively is a poorly-designed service.

A company designs services to satisfy or exceed customers' needs and requirements. But the company also has needs and requirements:

- To satisfy its stakeholders;
- To make a profit;
- To continue in business and develop.

If the services it designs cannot be delivered profitably, then it will fail.

Modularity

The design for delivery concept works to help companies to design services that can be offered effectively.

Back in the 1930s and 1940s, General Motors came to understand this concept. Very many of its cars were designed using main modules that were then packaged in different outer skins. We see the same happening today, with software companies developing key modules of code that then can be customised to give customer-specific offerings. By using tried and tested modules, a software company can significantly reduce service development time as well as reducing the complexity within the operations area when it comes to time to deliver the service.

Standardisation

If a company can standardise on a number of modules or sub-elements across its service range, significant savings can be made at the operations level.

Designers want to design – it is, after all, their basic function – but their creative talents are best used when they design using standardised elements or parts. The range of tools and methods available today means that any number of designers can design a service to meet a given specification, without any two of them using the same elements from the same source. It is fundamentally important to put some basic controls on the type and variety of components available for choice by the design team.

Click Count

Today many services are delivered electronically, over the Web. Service designers are focused on the 'click count': how many times a customer has to click with their mouse to achieve their objective. The widespread use of smart phones and tablets once again has challenged service developers to provide their service and content on even more restricted platforms, while still delivering a good customer experience. The fewer clicks, the better the opportunity for a higher quality customer experience to be delivered.

Design for Assembly

The previous point of reducing click count has an equally important application in the area of design for assembly.

By designing services with a view to how they will be delivered to customers, designers can have a significant impact on operational efficiency – for example, useful techniques to improve service performance include:

- Ensuring services can be assembled from existing offerings, avoiding the need to develop a new specification each time;
- Ensuring that equipment needed to deliver the service is located so that the elements that go along with a sale are to hand and easily accessed;
- Minimising the number of elements, or maybe even increasing them to enhance the customer's 'buying experience';
- Defining the format of delivery packaging to ensure that all customers have the same experience.

Foolproofing at the design stage can save large amounts of lost time and waste in the service delivery process. Design services so there is only one, obvious way to deliver them.

Design for Testing

The test function is quite often a bottleneck in an operation. Testing procedures can be difficult to formulate to ensure that the service or software is provided or developed to an acceptable level. Designers should design to allow for quick and effective testing.

Design for Process

Simplicity has been a constant thread running through the tools and techniques of LB.

When designing a new service, consideration should be given to how it will be delivered, to the physical processes required to get it to the customer. Unless specific technological requirements demand it, it is best to stick to tried and proven processes. Proven equipment can deliver with a degree of consistency not always obtainable from newer technologies.

Frequently, winning companies let a technology pass the experimental and first-rush stages before incorporating it as an integral element of their core processes.

Service Evaluation

It is important to know what is happening in your market. When a new service or offering is launched by competitors, it is very important that your staff get a good understanding of it as soon as possible. Many leading companies issue their sales staff with competitive analyses of their competitors' offerings.

Close scrutiny of competitors' service offerings can pay dividends for your company. You may see a new idea that, when modified or developed by your own staff, may lead to significant improvements and cost savings. The evaluation process should be organised and professionally carried out. Ideally, your own customers' requirements analysis should be used when examining competitive service offerings, to see where the competition stands in relation to your own features and characteristics:

By critically examining the features of competitive service offerings, you can ascertain how well your own service meets the customers' requirements.

When sales volumes are factored into the analysis, you can come to an understanding of the sensitivity of the market to different factors and features.

A simple analysis of what the customer places emphasis on could be a starting point for a re-examination of the interpretation of the customers' buying criteria, and possibly of service positioning in the market.

CONCLUSION

A well-designed service will:

- Perform as intended;
- Give a good customer experience;
- Continue to deliver as expected;
- Be easily and safely delivered at low cost, relatively speaking.

The following quotation aptly summarises the central concept of this chapter:

- **From Kenney and Florida (1993):** "At the core of the new model of innovation-mediated operations stands a set of fundamental changes in the organization of work at the point of delivery – a 'new shop floor' – which is geared toward harnessing and mobilising intellectual labour. Both the office floor and the R&D laboratory become a source of continuous innovation, productivity improvement, value creation, and capital accumulation".

17: Strategy & Implementation

Many books on business development start with strategy. They say that a business needs a strategy before it can develop. The Lean Service approach is different. It is based on the fact that most service businesses already have service offerings, assets and customers, its strategy is largely a given and so Lean Service is focused on helping to identify ways to meet and exceed competition levels within a sector by adopting good business practice. But there is still a definite need for strategy within a business applying a Lean Service approach.

STRATEGY

Business strategy can be likened to map reading. Before a map can be used effectively, it is essential to know the starting point, the destination and to be able to see the map and understand it, and to be able to work out a route. Business strategy provides the map for a business. By clearly identifying the starting point, say, using benchmarking as a diagnosis tool, and by stating an objective, the strategy can help to rally the efforts of all involved in a business to achieve that goal. If the strategic objectives of the business are not clearly stated, if they stay inside the heads of the management, then it is very difficult for others to know where the business is going and to work out how they are supposed to help get the business there.

A good strategic plan should include a mission or vision for the company that tells people the big picture.

Goals

Goals are results or objectives that need to be achieved. These need to be real and easily understood to act as clear targets for management and workers. As examples, these goals could be:

- To achieve x % per cent profitability;
- To make sales of €y per year;
- To be integrated into the local community.

An effective strategic plan needs to look internally at the company itself and externally at its customers, its competitors and the community or environment within which it operates (see **Figure 17.1**).

FIGURE 17.1: STRATEGY

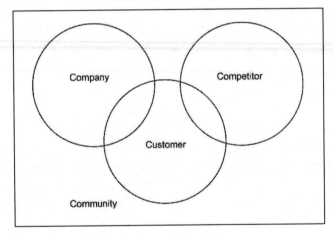

Customers

A business exists to meet the needs of its clients or customers. To do this effectively, it must know and understand those needs. It must understand:

- The difference between customers' needs and customers' wants;
- Who the customers are, what they buy, how often and in what quantities and varieties;

- Why customers do business with the company rather than with its competitors;

- How important individual customers are to the business – in terms of volume of sales and also profitability potential for growth and ease of doing business.

Often, a customer list has grown organically over time. The list may have a combination of low-value, high-maintenance customers as well as low-maintenance, high-value customers. The challenge for management, when preparing a strategic development plan for the business, is to maximise the benefit for the business from the customer base. This often involves a re-examination of the customer base with a move to re-focus sales efforts. By ranking customers using A, B, C analysis (see **Chapter 13**), often you can bring clarity to the sales function with improved overall benefit for the business.

Competition

Very few businesses function without competition. If competitors exist, it is important to be aware of who they are, what they are good at, what their products are and what features and weaknesses they exhibit. Effectively, competitors are trying to take your business away and so you need to defend yourself from them.

Learn about and study competitive services. Examining other people's solutions often can act as a stimulus to your own creativity, resulting in improved designs and increased customer satisfaction. Much of the advances in service design over the years has been based on learning from others and innovating.

Company

You must 'know yourself'. When working on a strategy, take the time to determine objectively the business' strengths and weaknesses. If people do not know what their business is capable of, then they may well set themselves unrealistic (too high or too low) targets and objectives. If they do not identify weaknesses at all, they may expose the business to failure or unsustainable stress.

The benchmarking process can help in identifying clearly and objectively the strengths and weaknesses of the business when compared to its sector and beyond. The SWOT technique, which is discussed shortly, provides a useful tool to assist in this process of self-identification.

Community

Businesses operate within a community and are affected by that community's laws and regulations. Similarly, the community's laws can provide opportunities for business. It is important that a business consider future changes in legislation, changes in demographics and changes in technology that may affect it as it develops its future strategy.

A number of tools have been developed to help companies understand their businesses and to help formulate a strategic plan.

SWOT Analysis

A SWOT analysis looks at the Strengths, Weaknesses, Opportunities and Threats facing a business.

SWOT analysis looks at the internal and external environment facing a business. On the internal front, the technique looks at the strengths of the business, seeking to reinforce them and to identify potential strategic advantage for the company. By identifying weaknesses, a business team can work to fix them, to find improvement to reduce their weaknesses.

On the external side, the company focuses on the opportunities that may exist, with a view to focusing on them and exploiting them as a concerted team. The team also can identify threats to their business and move to take counter-measures to protect the business.

A flipchart can be useful when doing a SWOT analysis, as it provides a highly visual way of capturing information. The usual way of representing the data is presented in **Figure 17.2**.

FIGURE 17.2: SWOT ANALYSIS

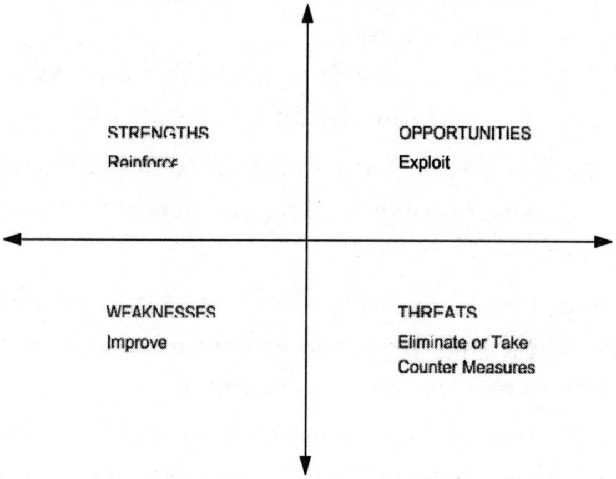

STRENGTHS
Reinforce

OPPORTUNITIES
Exploit

WEAKNESSES
Improve

THREATS
Eliminate or Take
Counter Measures

As the team examines its business, its customers, and its competition using the SWOT technique, real plans can be developed to make the business stronger.

The Service-Market matrix

The service-market matrix tool looks at the full service range of a business, with a view to clearly identifying which services have potential for growth and which are in decline. The tool uses a box system (see **Figure 17.3**), with all services located on the matrix.

FIGURE 17.3: THE SERVICE-MARKET MATRIX

	Lo	Hi
Hi (Current)	Wild Cats	Stars
Lo (Current)	Dead Dogs	Cash Cows

Earnings

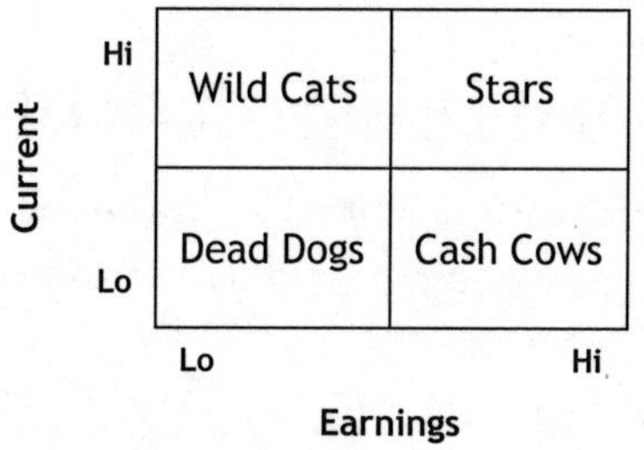

The use of this visual approach often helps a full business team to plan actions to maximise returns in the short to medium term or to

identify the need to develop new service offerings or innovations to secure the business into the future.

The matrix uses the following classifications to characterise services, with each classification leading to its own strategic plan:

- **Wild Cats:** Services with the potential to deliver high future earnings. Often unproven and maybe needing further development;
- **Dead Dogs:** Providing low present and future earnings potential. These may be 'bread and butter' services and would be unlikely to receive much investment;
- **Cash Cows:** Proven products with a limited life horizon. The strategy here is to maximise revenue with limited investment. Get as much from the service as possible;
- **Stars:** Proven current high earners with high potential future earnings. Significant investment would be made to maximise the life contribution of these services.

When a business uses the service-market matrix tool, it can usually identify where it should be focusing sales and marketing efforts, as well as engineering support and innovation time.

The use of the matrix also can be helpful in bringing attention to the life cycle of particular services or offerings. If there are no new services planned for the future, this fact can be clearly identified and action taken in time.

IMPLEMENTATION

The general in-company approach followed for Lean Service implementation is represented graphically in **Figure 17.4**.

The approach consists of:

- Business diagnostic;
- Lean Business (LB) – awareness and self assessment;
- Implementation planning;
- Step changes;
- Continuous improvement.

FIGURE 17.4: THE HIGH INTENSITY LEAN IN-COMPANY IMPLEMENTATION MODEL

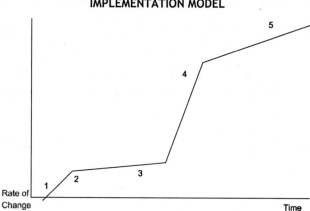

The approach is roughly based on Shewhart (1938, 1969) and the Lucas Business Systems approach (1991). It can be described as being the first five steps up an improvement ladder or stairs. From an overall perspective, the approach is best described as the first coil of an improvement spiral, rather than an improvement circle.

FIGURE 17.5: THE SPIRAL OF PERFORMANCE

Level 3 Tools & Techniques				
Process Benchmarking	The Five S's	Total Productive Maintenance	Overall Equipment Efficiency	Six Sigma
Business Excellence	Value Analysis & Management	Lean Production	Target Cost Management	

Level 2 Tools & Techniques			
Facilitated Assessment Benchmarking	Physical & Process Flow in the Office	Physical & Process Development	Production Control Systems
Saving Time in the Workplace	Maintenance	Practical Quality Tools	Team Building & Culture
Sales and Growing them	Financial Management	Supply Chain & Logistics	Innovation & Design
Business Strategy	Implementation		

Level 1 Tools & Techniques		
Process Mapping – What are you doing?	Check Sheets – What is going wrong	Teams – People working together to improve
Physical tracking – Where does material or paperwork go	Run Charts – Is it getting better or worse?	

Step 1: Business Diagnostic

"Before moving to a new land it is advisable to know where you are starting from".

The business diagnostic involves a review of key areas of the business: finance, marketing, selling, materials, management, R&D and in particular, operations.

The main objective of this phase is to identify problems facing the business. This review of the current business situation can yield new insights into the nature of its problems. Some shortcomings in the manner in which the business is managed may come to light at this stage. Sometimes early actions or 'quick hits' can achieve disproportionate gains, winning credibility for the team and management commitment for the more intensive improvement drive yet to come.

The starting point can be a simple benchmarking exercise to identify issues or areas of difficulty facing the business. When starting on an improvement activity, it is best to focus people's efforts on tangible problems or issues. An analysis of the current sales profile can help identify key products or customers (**Chapter 13**). An analysis of the key processes can help identify priority areas for action.

Step 2: Lean Business Awareness & Self Assessment

LB programmes generally are driven by the senior mangers of a business, which means that the senior managers must have a clear understanding of what LB involves in order to pass on their knowledge to the rest of the workforce. The key individuals involved need to understand the main principles of LB and, more importantly, appreciate how those principles can be best put to use in their own company.

Once the company has come to an understanding of these basic principles, it can compare the results of the diagnostic phase against these principles as a form of self assessment. This assessment can be used as a basis for the implementation plan for the company. This interpretation process of the basics of LB will lead to the planning and implementation phase.

Step 3: Implementation Planning

At this stage, the company has learned about LB and interpreted these principles in relation to real issues within the company. The company diagnostic phase has identified a number of potential areas for improvement. The combination of these two elements allows the company to move to create an implementation plan.

A successful implementation plan needs to be practical and flexible. Practical improvements achieved at an early stage of the implementation programme will have a very positive effect on the morale of all concerned. The plan should be balanced between detail and flexibility. It is generally better to err on the side of flexibility at the planning stage, as this leaves the way open to get the best out of the full team, both at management and at worker level, as the process continues.

Step 4: Step Change

At this juncture, the examination has taken place; the company has learnt about, and come to its own understanding of, LB. Planning has also taken place and it is now time to implement the changes.

One of the features of lean implementation is that, at this point in the process, changes begin taking place within the company. Generally, these changes arise from a concerted implementation push as the operation moves into a new gear.

This stage is generally the most exciting and interesting part of the LB programme, as employees see major changes and generally major improvements. However, this is also the time when the process is most likely to go wrong. Because the company is moving through a process of serious change, the reaction of staff to change must be carefully managed. It is at this point that the importance of the previous two steps – LB awareness and implementation planning – really come home to the company.

Step 5: Continuous Improvement

The initial stages of a LB programme will lead to a number of immediate improvements in the general operation of the company. It is important to remember, however, that the company will need to continue the improvement process into the future.

It is strongly recommended that the company prepare a plan at the outset of the programme to provide for training and on-going assessment and to ensure that the LB principles become ingrained in the company.

The Lean Network In-Company Implementation Model

A Lean Network approach has been developed by the authors in conjunction with Enterprise Ireland. It is an evolutionary approach, developed as a practical response to the requirements and resources of SMEs. The improvement model for this framework looks like a series of incremental improvement steps and involves on-going diagnostic analysis and improvement project identification throughout the project. The process is presented diagrammatically in **Figure 17.6**.

FIGURE 17.6: THE LEAN NETWORK IN-COMPANY IMPLEMENTATION MODEL

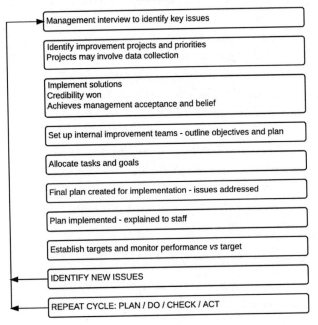

The Lean Network approach is modelled on the Japanese Kaizen, or small improvement steps, method. This approach is represented in **Figure 17.7** as a movement up the steps of a staircase. At each step, a business needs to identify its current state of performance as well as the key issues facing it. As time progresses, the issues are likely to change. As a business grows, it has requirements and faces challenges that were not present when it was smaller. Managers and staff need to identify this evolution and address the 'hierarchy of needs' of the business and work to create and develop the future business.

FIGURE 17.7: THE LEAN NETWORK IMPLEMENTATION MODEL - COMPANY LEVEL

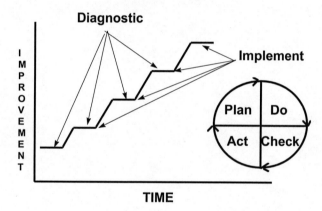

BRINGING IT ALL TOGETHER

A business' strategic plan provides the business with a clear direction for the future. It helps everybody involved with the business to understand how their efforts contribute to the overall goals and objectives of the operation.

Once the high level strategy has been defined, it is up to individual elements of the business to develop their strategies. Sales and marketing, design and operations as well as finance, all need to develop their individual strategies to deliver on the overall business strategy. This is an interactive process. The business strategy needs to be based on the abilities and resources of the business, and *vice versa*.

The business strategy provides a rallying call to ensure that all members of the business are working towards a common goal. Good implementation of a good strategy leads to good results.

Case Study 7: Lean in Professional Service Firms

The increasingly global dynamic of market opportunities to expand, the interconnectedness of organisations and an accelerated recognition of the importance of data and talent to successfully execute an organisation's strategic ambitions have changed the landscape for professional service firms.

In addition, increased regulatory oversight and the demand for value and efficient, focused and timely delivery of service has taken a step change since the global crisis in 2008, as regulators demand greater accountability and evidenced transparency and businesses look to grow bottom-line earnings off a mature and sluggish top-line outlook.

At Grant Thornton, we have been a strong advocate of the principles of Lean to ensure our continued relevance in a changed business landscape - both in our own organisation and in our clients. As knowledge workers, there is now greater demand than ever from clients for our insights – moving from a 'you did' to a 'we think' dynamic.

In particular, we critically assessed our audit process and have used evolving technologies to enable our services to be more targeted and delivered more efficiently and at an affordable and relevant price. Adopting the principles of Lean pushes us towards achieving the 'fifth quarter' – where we produce more from the same resources by changing and building the capability and capacity of our people and processes.

Grant Thornton in the UK, for example, has stratified some 2,500 audit tests into the three distinct areas of non-judgmental, judgmental and those requiring expert knowledge. Based on these insights, the firm is redesigning the flow, location, bundled technologies employed and appropriate competences of the organisation to make the firm more agile, thus creating opportunities for its people to leverage their knowledge and experiences to allocate this 'new' time profitably to where it can create the biggest impact.

Gaining trusted advisor status is the Holy Grail on the journey of successful professional service firms. Lean is a 'must have' companion for that journey.

Case Study 8: Lean in Service

Over the last three years, we have been rolling out Lean practices within Musgrave as part of our Continuous Improvement (CI) programme, which incorporates all office environments, our distribution centres, suppliers and our retail partners.

We strive to eliminate non-value add steps, while at the same time adding more value to the customer. In our office environments, lead times of key processes have reduced by over 50%, paper has been eliminated or dramatically reduced and non-value or business non-value reduced by 80%.

Increasing colleagues' understanding of Lean and CI was crucial to our success. We up-skilled all staff on specific Lean tools we felt were most relevant for our business. We changed one of our guiding principles to ensure that there was clear strategic alignment. We introduced three levels of improvement, so colleagues at all levels of the organisation were engaged.

We aimed to standardise core processes, with many departments implementing standard work. Our sales team have clear timeframes when we communicate with stores. We introduced visual management within our business and within our retail stores. Teams conduct regular huddles at visual boards so there is transparency of performance.

While still relatively early days on our CI journey, we have seen the benefits at every level of the organisation. While Lean initially might have been viewed as the preserve of manufacturing or operations, we have seen colleagues embrace tools such as value stream mapping when regularly implementing CI projects.

Level 3

Advanced Lean Service

18: Process Benchmarking

Process benchmarking is probably the most difficult type of benchmarking to do, although possibly the most beneficial, if it is done correctly.

Process benchmarking involves company staff in identifying a key issue for the business, mapping the internal process associated with that issue and identifying leading examples of how this process is handled in other businesses. These leading examples may be outside their own sector and in the private or public sectors. When leading organisations in the process have been identified, they are approached with a view to arranging a study mission.

The process benchmarking approach is often quite involved and can absorb significant amounts of time and money. The true benefit of process benchmarking is realised at the implementation stage, when the improvements identified are implemented back in your own company.

A business starting out on a process benchmarking exercise is focussing on achieving best practice within its operation. It wants, or needs, to be performing at the highest level. When looking for best practice, a benchmarking team is looking to identify a successful method to deliver a process. It is important to be sure that the method is proven to deliver results; it is not enough to look for a different method. If a benchmarked process is to be useful to a business, then it needs to be able to demonstrate clear benefits over the existing process.

However, it is very seldom that a process can be copied from one operation to another. Circumstances are often different – for example, interfacing processes and customer requirements can be different. It is essential to understand the fundamentals of the benchmarked process to enable effective adaptation of the process to meet specific business needs, without compromising the effectiveness of the benchmarked process.

HOW TO PROCESS BENCHMARK

The first, and possibly most important, step in process benchmarking is identifying *what process* to benchmark. It is essential to identify a process that is sufficiently significant to the sustainable competitiveness of your business that it warrants the dedication of resources to its improvement.

The second key step in the process is to identify *who* to benchmark with. It may seem ideal to benchmark your invoice processing with a world-leading company, but maybe the scale and scope of such a business is too big. Think carefully to identify who has significantly better process performance. It is not always necessary to chase 'best practice'; it often can be very sensible to look for 'better practice' first, learning about and implementing that before chasing best practice.

It is also worthwhile to think about how well the processes of others perform, to find measures of performance that can help you identify better and best practice operators.

A four-stage Process Benchmarking approach is presented in **Figure 18.1**, and described in the following sections.

FIGURE 18.1: THE PROCESS BENCHMARKING CYCLE

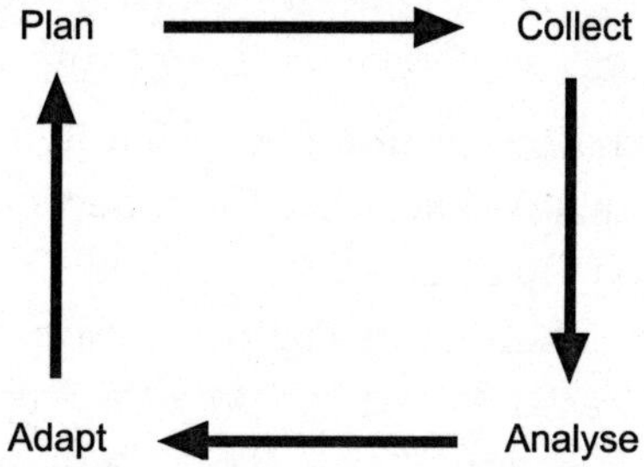

Stage 1: Plan

The first stage in a successful process benchmarking exercise is to plan the activity. This stage can be broken down into a number of elements:

- **Form a benchmarking team:** Ideally, select people who have experience of improvement activities, and who have knowledge of using the tools presented in Levels 1 and 2;

- **Document the selected process:** It is essential that the detail of the selected process is known and understood before going to examine other people's processes. The simple act of documenting the chosen process can lead to the identification of wastes and improvement opportunities. Fix these before going to look at other processes;

- **Establish the scope of the study:** The project needs to be clearly defined and achievable. If the scope is too broad, then the project may well be impossible to complete;

- **Define objectives for the process:** Set some targets that will challenge the team but that are likely to show a positive outcome for the effort;

- **Develop criteria for benchmark partners:** Who would be appropriate to benchmark with? Should they be in the same sector, or country? What size of business is appropriate?

- **Identify potential benchmark partners:** Think clearly about who would be interesting, stimulating and rewarding to visit. A number of benchmarking clubs exist where those interested in benchmarking work together to improve their operations;

- **Determine a data collection plan:** Identify some key measures and methods that will facilitate the collection of the right information to help understand the detail of the benchmarked processes. Work hard at this point, as careful identification of triangulated measures that can provide deep insights into good practice are very helpful. Try to find more than one measure for a practice, so that measures support or negate each other. If you find two independent measures that support each other, then it is likely that you have found good practice.

Stage 2: Collect

It is now time to start collecting data on the potential benchmark partners. It is useful, and polite, to learn as much as possible about potential partners before contacting them. Careful preparation will make it clear that this benchmark process is both professional and well thought-out. Potential partners will appreciate that the groundwork has been done and that there is a logic to their selection for, and participation in, the process.

A number of distinct steps are involved:

- **Carry out secondary research on the potential partners against the sort criteria:** What has been published about their operations or their processes? What is in the trade journals or business magazines? Is there academic research published about them?

- **Evaluate the research and finalise the potential partners list:** Research sources can often be helpful in confirming potential partners or in deciding to remove them from the list. Work to finalise the potential partner list.

- **Develop the data collection instrument:** The instrument or questionnaire must capture the basic information required to understand the practices, methods and techniques employed by the benchmark partners;

- **Pilot the data collection instrument internally:** Use the questionnaire internally, before sending it to any potential partners. Check to ensure that all questions are understood without additional explanation. Also check that the answers given to questions are understood and clear. Adjust the questionnaire if necessary;

- **Contact potential benchmark partners and enlist their participation:** The moment of truth. Potential partners must be contacted and enlisted to join the exercise;

- **Carry out site visits:** Conduct a detailed site visit to the chosen partners. Use the questionnaire and also keep notes of discussions. Share the workload during the site visit between the team members. Remember, two pairs of eyes are better than one, so use time on site to maximum effect;

- **Review site visit information:** After each visit, carry out a de-briefing session where each team member shares what they saw, heard and learned during the visit. Capture these insights. Also capture any outstanding questions that were not asked or answered during the visit or which arose following the de-briefing. Use telephone or email contact with the benchmark partner to address these questions.

Stage 3: Analyse

Having captured the basic information, it is essential to see what can be learned from the data, to turn it into information and potential benefit.

The steps here are:

- **Compare current in-house performance data to benchmark partners' data:** How does the internal operation compare with what was observed at the benchmark partners?

- **Identify operational best practice and enablers:** Typically, there will be some aspects of each of the benchmark partners' processes that are worth noting. It is unusual to find one single source of best practice. List out what appears to be the best combination of practices. Look to find the best grouping from all the benchmarked sites, including your own. It is important to understand whether there are any fundamental factors that are critical to the adoption of best practice in the sites visited. If these cannot be replicated in your workplace, it may be impossible to transfer best practice;

- **Develop an implementation plan and strategy:** What is to be implemented and how will it contribute to improving the core process? What level of resources or infrastructural change will be required to ensure the successful adaptation and adoption of best practice? Time spent at this stage of the process is often fundamental to assuring a successful outcome.

Stage 4: Adopt

Now comes time to start implementing the improvements at base. The steps are:

- **Implement the plan:** Take action, being aware of difficulties that may be encountered and being quick to respond to them. If staff have problems, work with them to find positive solutions. If their problems are ignored, it could result in the failure of the exercise as staff revert to the old ways. Also, by addressing and understanding problems with implementation, it is often possible to develop even better and more effective responses to the process problems. Adaptation and innovation at this stage often yield further improvements;

- **Monitor and report progress:** People need to see that their efforts to improve are being recognised. By monitoring progress over time, it will be possible to show either improvements achieved or problems encountered. Either way, everyone will be aware that the process is important to the business and that their efforts are appreciated;

- **Plan for continuous improvement:** When people have become comfortable with the new process, ask them where and how they think they can improve it further. This is particularly important for strategically significant processes. The simple act of asking whether the process can be improved further often yields results based on the accumulated experience of staff using the already improved process.

CONDUCTING A BENCHMARKING EXERCISE

Now let's look at some of the softer aspects, including some basic considerations, how one might find benchmark partners, some general causes for failure and success and finishing with a checklist for conducting a successful exercise.

Basic Considerations

There are a number of basic considerations involved with a process benchmarking exercise. These can be classified generally as relating to manners and practicalities.

The first of these points is reciprocity. It should go without saying that, if another business opens its doors to your team, then you should be prepared to return the favour. So, one should be careful and aware of this when considering who to approach. Reciprocity usually also extends to the sharing of general results identified in the study. It is normal for the lead company to create a final report on the full exercise and to circulate it to all businesses involved in the exercise.

When trying to decide on benchmark partners, try to identify partners whose operations or processes are similar to your own. If the process or business is too dissimilar, then it can be very difficult to convince others back at base that there are useful lessons to be learned.

Be careful in what metrics are chosen to measure performance. Be sure to try them out in your own operation first. Remember, metrics often can be manipulated by capable managers. A call centre that focuses on the number of calls answered will get very different overall results than one that focuses on the numbers of calls resolved.

The objective of a process benchmarking exercise is to gain a true and deep understanding of the benchmarked processes. If only a superficial knowledge is gained, it is very unlikely that any real insights will be gained and even less likely that any true value will be achieved. Remember the benchmarking code of conduct. Do not look where you are not supposed to. Do not ask commercially sensitive questions. Do not risk compromising yourself or your business.

Causes of Failure and Success

Experience has shown that there are a number of causes that can lead to either a successful or a failed benchmarking exercise.

Causes of failure include:

- Own processes not properly documented;
- Performance gap not identified;

- Scope of project too big – broad *vs.* deep;
- Not learning from what is available (renouncing the expert);
- Looking for best practice, when better practice may be a sufficient target;
- Lack of management support;
- Refusing to see and / or believe internal weaknesses or other organisation's superior performance.

Causes of success include:

- Senior management as process owners;
- Concept of continuous improvement in place;
- The team understands the benchmarking process;
- Timing is right – for the company and its benchmarking partners.

In every successful process benchmarking project, the project:

- Has top management commitment;
- Focuses on key business issues;
- Supports overall business improvement strategy
- Demonstrates benefits outweigh costs
- Project allocates necessary human resources
- The people involved have the necessary knowledge
- There are measurable and time-based objectives
- There is a plan to show what is to be benchmarked.

Specifically, the plan:

- Shows how and from where data will be collected;
- Shows how and where "best practice" could be identified;
- Defines how to monitor the implementation of best practices;
- Shows a clear timescale for each step;
- Predicts best and worst case results;
- Defines a review of achievements.

19: "To Infinity & Beyond"

Your business has now mastered the fundamental tools and techniques of Lean Business. It is competing well at national level and has started to sell in the world market. So, what comes next?

By this point, both managers and staff should be aware that there are some really strong operators on the world stage. They should be aware that they have achieved significant improvements within their operations, through their own efforts. They also should be painfully aware that the real challenge has just begun. They will be running with the big dogs now! If they have successfully managed to reach the international stage, they will be willing and able to move to the next levels of challenge.

A business should now be seeking to make continuous improvement a bedrock of the operation. Management and staff must realise that they have two jobs to do:

- The 'day job';
- Finding ways to improve the effectiveness of the operation.

Managers can achieve real benefits for all by building this realisation and fostering the enthusiasm of all concerned with the business. This includes both suppliers and customers.

This chapter provides some insight into some advanced Lean tools and techniques as a taster. In this way, managers will have the opportunity of considering which approach may help them in addressing the key strategic challenges facing their operations.

Excellence is no accident, it is the result of strong leadership identifying a goal and harnessing the combined strengths and abilities of other people and the available assets to achieve that goal.

By focusing people's attention on stretch targets, the world's best companies build their people through constant innovation. These tools and techniques support this effort. It is not magic – it is hard work – but it is rewarding for all.

THE FIVE Ss

The Five Ss is a Japanese approach designed to focus attention on the basics of cleanliness and organisation. The phrase 'a place for everything and everything in its place' goes a long way to explaining the Five S system. The approach is founded on the principle that it is very difficult, if not impossible, to improve performance without order and cleanliness. The system focuses, therefore, on achieving effective workplace organisation, a clearly laid-out and well-defined work environment and achieves waste reductions while simultaneously improving quality and safety.

The Five Ss relate to five Japanese words:

- **Seiri – Sorting out:** Keep only those items in a work area that are necessary. If parts, components or tools are only needed occasionally, keep them in a storage area, not in the work area. If items are no longer needed, then recycle or dispose of them. Seiri tackles the habit of keeping things because they might be useful, someday. By reducing clutter, it is easier to find what is required. Also, valuable space can be released for new projects at minimal cost;

- **Seiton – Systematic arrangement:** The shadow board is a classic example of Seiton, the search for the most effective arrangement of tools and materials to have them available in the most efficient way. Mark the floor areas or storage areas to highlight where and how materials, finished goods and tools are to be stored and handled for maximum efficiency;

- **Seiso – Spic and span:** Clean the work place and keep it clean. Cleaning the workspace often leads to a safer working environment, as less clutter and clear passages make it easier and safer to complete work. Cleaning can also be seen as providing a basic level of inspection. If leaks, cracks, breakages or misalignments are detected early, then remedial action can take place before damage is done – for example, if you see that a milk carton is damaged as you place it into the fridge, you can do something then that will avoid the later loss of time cleaning up afterwards;

- **Seiketsu – Standardising:** Set the new standard. Unless the new, clean and organised standard is defined, then human nature will ensure that things revert to the old ways. Involve people in setting and raising the standard further;

- **Shitsuke – Self discipline or Perseverance:** Keep with the standard, and ensure that people keep their areas at, or above, the defined standard. People will internalise the standard through perseverance, until it becomes the norm.

The 5 S system is very basic, but also quite powerful.

Remember, managers set the standard for a business. If a low standard is acceptable, then that is what is achieved. If a high standard is the target, then it too will be achieved.

SIX SIGMA

The Six Sigma approach was developed by Motorola Corporation, as part of its efforts to achieve corporation-wide excellence. It is now used by Motorola as a key driver in its continuous improvement activity. General Electric, under Jack Welsh, adopted Six Sigma as a means of driving and supporting its relentless pursuit of performance improvement based on facts. The Six Sigma tools were used in such diverse areas as finance, administration and back office support functions as well as in the production of gas turbines.

The approach builds upon the concepts of quality management tools and brings a high degree of rigour to their wide-spread application and use. The approach is used to focus a business on customer requirements, understanding processes within an operation and ensuring that they are aligned. It is centred on the rigorous use of analytical methods and requires appropriately timed intervention and action to address issues identified and for the implementation of responses and counter- measures.

The Six Sigma approach is centred around the reduction of variability within a process. As the focus is on customers' wants and needs, projects initiated under the Six Sigma approach start with the identification of a customer issue and end with the resolution of that issue. Effort is expended to make processes as near perfect as is humanly possible.

The Sigma refers to a statistical measure known as 'standard deviation'. By reducing the variability in a process, it is possible to reduce very significantly the opportunity for the process to be outside specification. If the process is not outside specification, then the customer gets what they want and require. In real terms, if a process is running at Six Sigma levels, then a fault or defect occurs no more than 3.4 times in every million items.

Motorola also developed the DMAIC methodology to support the roll-out of the Six Sigma concept:

- **Define** the problem and the project to address it;
- **Measure** and gather basic data as the starting point for the project;
- **Analyse** the data, look for and identify root causes of defects;
- **Improve** the process by addressing the key causes;
- **Control** the process to ensure that it does not revert to the old ways.

The approach is highly disciplined and provides staff with the tools to manage and improve a process or product. It can be likened to using quality tools on steroids. Motorola regards it not purely as a quality methodology but rather as a way of doing business.

BUSINESS EXCELLENCE

The European Foundation for Quality Management (EFQM) provides businesses and organisations with a non-prescriptive framework to help them achieve true excellence (**www.efqm.org**). Because the model is non-prescriptive, it recognises the fact that there is no one best way to improve a process. Instead, it provides a number of basic concepts that are deemed to be fundamental to the achievement of excellence.

These fundamental concepts are, according to the EFQM:

- **Results orientation:** A key driver for the organisation needs to be a focus on achieving results, results that exceed the expectations of all stakeholders and that, in fact, delight them;

- **Customer focus:** Excellent organisations place significant emphasis on the achievement and delivery of sustainable customer value through a customer-focused orientation;

- **Leadership and constancy of purpose:** For an organisation to excel, it must have leadership of a high calibre – leadership that sees beyond the ordinary, that identifies and communicates a vision for the organisation that all can subscribe to. This vision needs to be coupled with resolve and constancy of purpose – it is not good enough to give in at the first signs of adversity. Leaders excel by creating and sharing a vision, and then leading an organisation to its achievement;

- **Management by process and facts:** Businesses are complex, it is important to understand the distinct processes and systems at work and to identify and develop coherent inter-relationships and effective management and improvement processes. The capturing of the facts of a business can lead to informed decisions being taken throughout an organisation, at the most appropriate level;

- **People involvement and development:** By involving and developing their people's capabilities and experience, businesses will maximise their contribution, flexibility and abilities;

- **Continuous learning, innovation and improvement:** The market is constantly evolving and changing. To be competitive, an organisation needs to adopt the approach of continuous improvement, building on an on-going basis its learning and innovation approaches and constantly seeking improvements;

- **Partnership development:** Leading companies constantly look for value-adding partnerships in an effort to add value to their client interactions;

- **Corporate social responsibility:** The best organisations go beyond the basic minimum legal demands made of them. They seek to understand and develop their position within society and their contribution to it.

The Business Excellence Model developed by the EFQM consists of nine criteria, presented in **Figure 19.1**. These are broken down into five 'enablers' and four 'results'. The enablers relate to what an organisation does, how it operates, its internal processes, while the results deal with what is achieved, the outputs. Detail of the model can be obtained from the web site (**www.efqm.org**).

FIGURE 19.1: THE EFQM MODEL

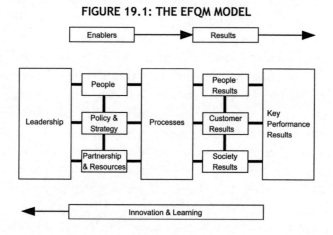

The original Business Excellence Model was heavily biased towards the needs and resources of large organisations. The EFQM continues to work to develop its SME-oriented model to bring excellence to small and medium-sized companies.

VALUE MANAGEMENT, ANALYSIS & ENGINEERING

The Value 'family' covers a framework or approach that relies on a systematically-applied team-based approach to identifying and enhancing the value offered by a service.

The approach is function-oriented, seeking to understand where the costs and values of individual functions are located. By focusing on the cost / value equation in functional terms, an optimised balance of cost, performance and quality is achieved. The approach was pioneered by Lawrence D Miles and much of his material is archived at University of Wisconsin-Madison (**www.wisc.edu/wendt/miles/**).

In general terms, Value Management (VM) is not a single method but an amalgam of methods brought together in a framework to achieve optimised value and function. The VM approach uses a closed feedback loop from the marketplace back to the system designers, ensuring that experience gained from the marketplace is integrated into evolutionary and future design work. In the software area there is quite a widespread adoption of the concept of 'Minimum Viable Product', where features are presented to the market in a continuous stream, allowing the software designing company to understand very quickly market place feedback. This close link with the market ensures the true value that the customer perceives is captured and enhanced during the development process.

The VM approach can be used on a project-by-project basis; however, companies that have championed the approach at senior management level have achieved major results by adopting a more strategic than project-based view.

The approach follows a systemised route now outlined.

Steps in VM

The VM Steering Group

A steering group is formed with the objective of identifying the strategic areas of the business that will be tackled by VM. This group is often supported by an experienced, external VM facilitator. It is also normal that at least one member of the steering group has experience in using VM to act as a conduit to the other members of the group.

Identifying VM Priorities

It is useful and important to identify key challenges facing the business, based on the strategic analysis of the steering group. As time and resources are limited, it is essential to prioritise key areas that are of high importance to the current and future success of the operation. These prioritised areas will provide direction when it comes to identifying specific VM projects.

Identifying VM Projects

The prioritised challenge areas facing the business have been identified. It is now time to look for and choose projects that can have an impact on improving the business by reducing cost and increasing value.

It should be clear that choosing an achievable project is a good way to introduce VM to a business, rather than tackling a very large or difficult project first.

Performing VM Projects

The prioritised list of projects to be tackled has been developed, based on business needs.

Each project now requires a 'job plan', consisting of:

- **Planning:** Good planning usually leads to success. VM uses planning to:
  - o Set the project objectives;
  - o Identify relevant team members;
  - o Capture the base information for the exercise;
  - o Discuss the project and consult with the staff;
  - o Plan a time line for specific actions;
  - o Identify whether there is a need for professional assistance;

- **Information Gathering:** The data relating to the project needs to be gathered to provide the project team with an objective starting point for their exercise;

- **Analyse the data and project parameters / objectives:** One of the most powerful VM tools is that of Function Analysis – identifying what exactly a part, component, sub-system or system actually does. Since a single item often performs a number of functions, it is essential to understand the functionality of all elements of a system before moving to change it. Flowcharting and process analysis tools are useful in assisting the mapping and understanding of processes;

- **Creative phase:** Enhancing the value. Techniques such as brainstorming are used in a structured way to challenge the team to identify potential improvements, radical changes, enhancements and cost savings for the project. Alternative methods, means and solutions are actively sought;

- **Evaluating:** The body of ideas created in the previous phase need to be evaluated to identify which are most likely to succeed. The ideas are prioritised under three headings: cost or saving, time to implement and general practicality;

- **Reporting:** Project teams report back to the Steering Group on their suggested solutions. These reports should be presented as business cases. Financial support material for suggested investments should accompany the reports, if appropriate;

- **Implementing:** Proposals that have passed the reporting stage and accepted for implementation need to be acted upon;

- **Follow-up phase:** VM is focused on Value, by reducing costs, increasing functionality and meeting customer needs and requirements. It is very important to carry out follow-up, to ensure that the expected results of projects are realised.

The VM approach focuses the minds of all concerned on the true value of their products or services. The use of a structured approach helps ensure that the creative and innovative phases of an operation operate within the strategic plan of the business, with the objective of delivering real customer value.

20: Practice to Perform

It seems very obvious to say that if you do the right thing (Practice), you will achieve the right result (Performance). In the late 1990s, academic research lead by Professor Chris Voss of the London Business School proved this linkage for business. A positive link was found between the practices that businesses employed and the level of performance that they achieved. This is a significant find for business. You can now be assured that, if you invest time and effort in adopting best practice, you will get a business reward.

In 2000, an Irish study compared 180 Irish SMEs against the results of thousands of European SMEs. The results of this study were published as the *Made in Ireland* report (Enterprise Ireland). **Figure 20.1** looks at the results of this report and compares them with European data.

FIGURE 20.1: PERCENTAGE OF COMPANIES IN EACH MICROSCOPE CLASSIFICATION

	UK	Belgium	Italy	Rest of Europe	Ireland
At Risk	1	7	39	0	4
Vulnerable	18	6	8	14	27
Inefficient	37	26	31	31	23
Contenders	39	49	2	48	39
World Class	0	0	0	4	1

Source: *Made in Ireland* Report, Enterprise Ireland.

An analysis of the figures shows that Ireland has a large tail of companies in the lower regions, with a significant number either At

Risk or Vulnerable. This long tail of poor performers seems to explain why Ireland ranks 15th in terms of European productivity. If we are to address this situation, it is important that Irish SMEs move to adopt best practice.

CONCLUSION

This book has presented a picture of the challenges facing Irish business, as well as a picture of some possible answers to the many issues facing today's managers. The use of objective benchmarking provides people with clear indications of how good they are and also where they need to focus their improvement efforts.

The basic Lean Business tools outline key practices that have proven helpful to many Irish businesses in their efforts to improve. The tools have worked well in very many sectors, in very many different sized businesses, in every corner of the island.

The three levels of implementation have presented a step-by-step guide to the effective use of these tools.

The challenge now facing Irish business is: **Are we mature enough to take on the task of really competing with the best?**

If we are committed to operating at even higher levels of performance, then we are almost assured of success. We are intelligent, well-educated, creative people who can and do work hard. The future of our country and our children rests with us. Are we up to the challenge?

Appendix 1: Self Assessment Questionnaire

Introscope is a simple benchmarking tool, designed to introduce people working in a wide variety of businesses and organisations to the power of benchmarking.

Using a sample of questions drawn from some of the best available benchmarking tools, Introscope invites you (perhaps with a few colleagues) to assess some of your organisation's key practices and performance aspects against a model of 'best practice', and to discover how your assessments compare to those of hundreds of other organisations. Start by confirming the scope of your assessment, which could be a department, site or the whole organisation – it will work at any of these levels, so long as you are consistent.

If you find Introscope and its outputs useful, ask about the range of more sophisticated benchmarking tools from which you can select one suitable for your needs. You will have to invest a little more effort, but you are likely to find this well worthwhile as benchmarking results help you to shape your improvement plans with confidence.

HOW TO SCORE

You choose the statement most appropriate to your organisation / site and this gives you a score – the number in the grey band above, 1,3, or 5. Sometimes, you may feel that your organisation is between two statements. In this case you choose the number between the two statements, 2 or 4.

If you see differences across the organisation, where some areas are more advanced than others, it is best to assess an average position. For example, a pilot implementation does not warrant the maximum score of five. We seek to assess the your position TODAY, not where it will be when current plans and projects deliver the results you expect. Benchmarking will only ever be of value to you if assessments are true reflections of the practices and performance of the organisation as it is NOW.

THE INTROSCOPE QUESTIONS

Introscope questions are drawn from the longer questionnaire scripts used by three of the best available benchmarking tools:

- Service Microscope
- The Micro Business Review
- Service PROBE.

		1	3	5
1	Role of leadership in developing customer-focused culture	Little attention paid by top management	Supported by top management, delegated down	Top management visibly promotes and actively participates
2	Service meeting customer needs	Service does not consistently meet the customer needs	Service generally meets customer needs	Service produces results that consistently meet and exceed customer needs
3	Quality performance, relative to sector	Poor overall quality record, compared to sector	Achieved levels about equal to the sector standard	Achieved a reputation for excellence in quality services that is notable in the sector and significantly better than the competition
4	The time it takes	We lose some business because it takes longer than customers want to wait to deliver our services	Our speed is neither a strength nor a weakness for us in gaining business	We win business because we are quicker than the competition

		1	3	5
5	Quality mind-set	Problems will happen. Deal with customer complaints	Inspection and control with some data collection	Total quality mindset. Quality is everyone's job, and employees take ownership of process
6	Training and education	*Ad hoc*, no plan	Some skills and development training for all employees	More than 5% of each employee's time devoted to training with strong emphasis on quality
7	Problem-solving	Crisis mindset, confusion, finger-pointing	System for recognising and responding to problems, emphasis on process not people, teamwork	Problems viewed as opportunities for further improvement, employees empowered to correct
8	Employee morale	Pressure and stress, anxiety about future, cynicism	Stability, *status quo* or moderate progress, occasional stress situations	Controlled environment, growth opportunities, consensus on direction, optimism and confidence
9	Innovativeness	No recent innovations in service concept and process	Regular innovations in service and an occasional major breakthrough innovation	Many innovations; recognised as a leading innovator in segment
10	New service design and development process	No identifiable process for improving existing services or for new service development	*Ad hoc* basis; services developed and improved regularly but no set process	Formal and reproducible process for developing new and enhancing existing services
11	Management of business processes	No attention to business processes (for example, customer billing process)	Key processes defined and mapped; initial steps taken toward redesigning and improving these processes	Key business processes managed and redesigned where needed; process owners in place; process performance measured

		1	3	5
12	**Reliability of equipment and systems**	We only maintain things when they break down. Perhaps this is why we have frequent problems with equipment (computers; equipment used in delivery of our services)	Maintenance is carried out to the maker's instructions. We plan time for this in order to reduce the risk of failure. We have adequate data security and back-up procedures	We take maintenance seriously. We try to anticipate problems and are prepared to invest time/money to prevent them. The people who use the equipment day to day take responsibility for looking after it
13	**Housekeeping**	Cluttered and disruptive	Organised	Clean, orderly, minimum work-in-progress, self-maintained, always 'tour ready'
14	**Relationships with Suppliers**	Many vendors, seek low bid, no certification programme	A few certified suppliers, Just-in-Time for hardware and consumables	Partnerships with certified suppliers, Just-in-Time deliveries, involved in service and process design improvements
15	**Operating costs**	Operating costs greater than the competition	Competitive	Operating costs lowest in the industry
16	**Level of customer satisfaction**	Customer expectation often not met; some customer complaints	Little customer dissatisfaction; expectations met, but rarely exceeded	Many delighted customers; customers will enthusiastically recommend the service/product to others; expectations often exceeded
17	**Customer Satisfaction measurement**	Limited measurement of customer satisfaction	Regular measurement of customer satisfaction in large, broad-based samples of customers	Careful identification of the dimensions of customer satisfaction by segment, using a broad range of measurement tools

		1	3	5
18	**Performance measurement and reporting**	By costs and sales volumes (accounting/ finance-driven)	By costs and non-financial measures of process outcomes	Using multiple measures (a balanced scorecard such as customer satisfaction, market share, employee morale and financial)

Organisation's name:

Unit or Site name:

Type of Organisation:

Number of people working in the organisation:

Address (full postal):

Post code:

Telephone (and code):

Fax (and code):

e-mail address:

Name and position of person responding:

Date:

Name of adviser & organisation:

All information in this questionnaire is confidential.

Your answers will be used by your advisor / advisory organisation to give you confidential feedback, which should help you to develop an action plan. The information about your organisation's practices / performance will also be used as an anonymous contribution to future benchmarking analysis.

© University of Northumbria at Newcastle 2001

Introscope has been developed by the Centre for Business Excellence at Northumbria University with support from the PROBE partnership, and is managed on their behalf by Comparison International.
www.cbe.unn.ac.uk www.comparisoninternational.com

Appendix 2: Facilitated Assessment & Comparison Tools

In **Chapter 8**, we considered Facilitated Assessment Benchmarking (FAB). In Europe today, two leading FAB tools exist:

- **Microscope / Probe** – a largely qualitative approach, focusing mainly on the practices and systems businesses use: www.comparisoninternational.com;

- **BenchmarkIndex** – a largely quantitative system, focused on capturing the hard measures of performance being achieved: www.benchmarkindex.com.

These tools have many thousands of benchmark data sets captured from businesses in Europe and beyond, in America, Australia and the Far East.

THE MICROSCOPE / PROBE CLASSIFICATION SYSTEM

The work of Professor Chris Voss and others resulted in the generation of a six-level classification system for companies dependent on their benchmark results. This system is now presented, along with the challenges facing a company if they are located in each classification:

- **Group A: Lean – Staying in Front:** This group is representative of leading companies, they need to focus on building global capability, achieving rapid time to market, exploiting know-how of all partners, achieving a step change in costs. They also need to focus on providing their customers with mass customisation and be able to achieve environmental differentiation. In short, they need to focus on new ways to delight their customers;

- **Group B: Contenders – En Route:** These companies have many of the characteristics of the leading companies and are well placed to reach full Lean status, they need to aim for 'delighted' customers, to strive to achieve market driven quality. To work to improve their operations using the EFQM / Baldrige templates. They need to focus on getting employee involvement and building an ethos of social and environmental responsibility. In short, they need to focus on service excellence;

- **Group C: Promising – Inhibited:** This group has a number of definite problems to overcome, quite often typified by poor management buy-in and commitment to continuous improvement. They have to build executive commitment, develop a flat organisation, and move to achieving employee empowerment, building their skills and developing effective training. They need to focus on building teamwork between their staff. They should be using benchmarking and introducing measurement and incentives to help guide them to improved performance;

- **Group D: Inefficient – Seeming to get 'Something for Nothing':** This group appears to be getting 'something for nothing'. An example of this could be in terms of delivered quality. They exhibit high delivered product quality, often without the benefit of a quality system, but quite often at the expense of full product final inspection rather than through the use of high quality processes. This high level of final inspection adds unnecessary cost to the product and the operation. They need to focus on developing a quality vision, building their customer and supplier partnerships. They need to tackle the problems of eliminating unnecessary cost from their operations and move towards a feeling of business process ownership among their staff. They need to focus on achieving effectiveness and efficiency;

- **Group E: Vulnerable – Where to Start?:** Probably the companies with the biggest problems, they are faced with the issue of recognising there is a crisis. They suffer from poor executive vision and lack a customer satisfaction focus. They tend to have little or no employee involvement and have major opportunities for process improvement. They need to focus on introducing control and predictability into their operations;

- **Group F: At Risk:** These companies are faced with the question of survival before attempting to improve.

Appendix 3: Sources of Further Information

Anon. (2001). *Made in Ireland Report*, Dublin: Enterprise Ireland, 2001.

Browne, S. (1996). *Strategic Manufacturing for Competitive Advantage: Transforming Operations from Shop Floor to Strategy*, Upper Saddle River, NJ: Prentice Hall.

Fortin, O. (2000). *The Irish Economic Boom: Facts, Causes and Lessons*, paper prepared for Industry Canada.

Hayes, R. & Pisano, G. (1994). 'Beyond World Class: The New Manufacturing Strategy', *Harvard Business Review*, January-February, pp. 77-86.

Kanter, R. (1991). 'Managing Change in Innovative Organizations' in Shetty, Y. & Buehler, V. (eds), *The Quest for Competitiveness*, New York: Quorum.

Kenney, M. & Florida, R. (1993). *Beyond Mass Production*, New York: Oxford University Press.

Maskell, B. (1989). Performance Measurement for World Class Manufacturing', *Management Accounting*, Vol.67, Iss.5, pp.32-33.

mu.motorola.com/ : Six Sigma information.

National Competitiveness Council (2000). *Annual Competitiveness Report 2000*, Dublin: Forfás.

Peters, T. & Waterman, R., (1982). *In Search of Excellence*, New York: Harper & Row.

Teerlink, R. & Ozley, L. (2000). More than a Motorcycle: The Leadership Journey at Harley-Davidson, Boston: Harvard Business School Press.

www.benchmarkindex.com: Benchmark Index.

www.benchmarking-in-europe.com: European Benchmarking Information.

www.comparisoninternational.com: Microscope Benchmark.
   www.dti.gov.uk/mbp/: Management Best Practice site of
   Department Trade and Industry, UK.
www.efqm.org: European Foundation for Quality Management.
   www.enterprise-ireland.com : Support for developing indigenous
   industry.
www.eujapan.com: EU Japan Centre for Industrial Co-operation.
www.excellence-ireland.ie: Excellence Ireland, Irish focal point for
   business excellence, quality and hygiene marks.
www.irishbenchmarkingforum.com: Irish Benchmarking information.
www.jipm.or.jp: Japanese Institute for Plant Maintenance.
www.onbusiness.ie/ndm.
www.wisc.edu/wendt/miles/: Value Engineering resource.

Index

OAK TREE PRESS

Oak Tree Press develops and delivers information, advice and resources for entrepreneurs and managers. It is Ireland's leading business book publisher, with an unrivalled reputation for quality titles across business, management, HR, law, marketing and enterprise topics. NuBooks is its recently-launched imprint, publishing short, focused ebooks for busy entrepreneurs and managers.

Oak Tree Press occupies a unique position in start-up and small business support in Ireland through its standard-setting titles, as well as training courses, mentoring and advisory services.

Oak Tree Press is comfortable across a range of communication media – print, web and training, focusing always on the effective communication of business information.

OAK TREE PRESS
E: info@oaktreepress.com
W: www.oaktreepress.com / www.SuccessStore.com.